This book isn't just a game-char̲ for innovators. Tom Pullen ma̲ innovation process, offering pragᵢₙₐₜᵢc, step-by-step guidance that addresses every critical hurdle. With his potent 'power questions' and engaging 'mini-missions', Tom delivers an unparalleled, actionable roadmap to becoming a truly exceptional innovator. Prepare to be inspired and equipped to innovate like never before!

Christophe Perthuisot
Chief Research & Innovation Officer
Moët Hennessy

Innovation can feel messy and overwhelming — yet it's a growth imperative for every company. *INNOVATOR* cuts through the complexity with a clear, human-centred roadmap that works in any organization. It's a truly didactic and practical playbook — valuable for team members and senior leaders alike. Essential for anyone who wants to lead change and deliver growth.

Jonathan Reeves
Senior Vice President
Global Head of R&D and Innovation, Opella

Tom Pullen's book brilliantly demystifies innovation, with a wonderfully clear 10-step process at its heart. It's packed with real-world examples, sharp insights, and practical tools you can put to work straight away — whatever your role.

Dave Robinson
Customer Strategy Director, Virgin Red

Innovation has become the 'must-have' for business differentiation and growth. If you're looking for concrete ways to enhance your innovation efforts, this book delivers. Knowing Tom Pullen's work, I am confident that the practical and actionable strategies he presents have been thoroughly tested.

Alicia Mansour, PhD, EMBA
Director of Innovation & Decarbonization, Veolia

For all those who live the thrill and tension of innovating inside a company, *INNOVATOR* reads like a compass in the fog, offering clear, actionable steps to innovate with speed and confidence. Simple, relevant and surprisingly powerful, this is the guide you'll want to equip your team of innovation heroes with.

Ilse Danes
Former Director of Growth Strategies
& Innovation, McCain Foods

Many professionals believe that innovating requires building a large and complex system — endless discussions, time-consuming workshops, and over-engineered testing phases — forgetting what truly matters: solving problems worth solving. In *INNOVATOR*, Tom Pullen offers a powerful yet simple framework that helps teams move from intent to action, reduce risk, create value, and bring new solutions into reality.

Baptiste Hediard
Senior Product Manager, Decathlon

Vision and collective commitment may ignite innovation, but without a carefully orchestrated plan they almost never deliver the outcomes that truly matter.

INNOVATOR offers far more than a simple methodology: it provides a clear, step-by-step guide to transforming strategy into growth — deceptively simple and undeniably effective.

Guillaume Robin
Head of E-commerce
& Accelerating Channels, Ferrero

A constantly changing world requires all of us to rethink, redesign and innovate as we go. The ability to innovate is a vital superpower in our complex world — and this book unpacks the what and the how with vivid examples, a clear process and practical steps. Whatever your business or role, read this compelling, well-written guide to the 10 simple steps to help you and your team innovate — and then put them into practice.

Kathryn Bishop, CBE FRSA
Non-executive Director and Associate Fellow
Author of *Board Talk*

INNOVATOR offers an insightful and pragmatic framework that is easy to adopt. Tom Pullen succeeds in capturing the essential elements without oversimplification. This book is full of inspirational illustrations and examples that reflect the author's extensive experience. I highly recommend it — and thank him for this book that truly fills a gap.

Sihem BenMahmoud-Jouini
Professor at HEC Paris, and Director of the
Innovation & Entrepreneurship specialization,
Executive MBA

No doubt: this book is destined to become both a reference and a bestseller in the field of innovation. It will prove just as valuable whether you are driving product and service innovation or advancing innovation in sustainable development. With *INNOVATOR*, innovation doesn't just become easier — it becomes a daily habit.

Marc Gillmann
Director of Entrepreneurship & Innovation
École Polytechnique

INNOVATOR is highly readable and full of practical frameworks that guide readers through the entire innovation journey. I can strongly recommend this book as an indispensable resource.

Alex Pickering
Lecturer in Marketing
Goldsmiths, University of London

In a time of constant change, *INNOVATOR* by Tom Pullen offers an original, robust and visual framework for innovating. A great read!

Christine Baldy-Ngayo, PhD
Director of Lifelong Learning at EPITA

For the innovators
— and those just beginning their journey

TOM PULLEN

INNOVATOR

10 simple steps to
innovate
with speed, scale
and confidence

First published in Great Britain by Practical Inspiration Publishing, 2026

9781788607704 (paperback)
9781788607698 (hardback)
9781788607711 (ebook)

EU GPSR representative: LOGOS EUROPE, 9 rue Nicolas Poussin, LA ROCHELLE 17000, France Contact@logoseurope.eu

Want to bulk-buy copies of this book for your team and colleagues? We can customize the content and co-brand *INNOVATOR* to suit your business's needs.

Please email info@practicalinspiration.com for more details.

Practical Inspiration
Publishing

Contents

PART 3: INNOVATOR IMPACT

Introduction

Once upon a time, 'innovation' referred to a quirky team tucked away in a corner of the office, playing with sticky notes. Fast forward to today, and it's the most critical capability for *anyone* serious about being successful in business. And, given that you picked up this book, that likely includes you.

There's no doubt about it – innovation is here to stay as a business priority. It fuels growth, keeps established companies alive in a world now moving at the supersonic speed of startups, and powers progress across society. Innovation isn't a nice-to-have anymore: it's a strategic imperative to stay relevant, resilient and fit for the future.

And whilst innovation may conjure up images of high-tech products or revolutionary technologies, there's one thing that we often forget: that no innovation exists without people. Or, more precisely, without innovators: those people who have the capability and confidence to magically turn ideas into impact.

Does that sound like you? Maybe not. Maybe, like most people, innovating successfully feels like a nearly impossible challenge: complex, slow and risky. Maybe the idea of speaking to customers makes you uneasy. Maybe you're unsure about how to generate original ideas. And, even if you do, maybe the thought of them failing stops you before you even start.

If that sounds familiar, it is certainly not your fault. Most of us were never taught how to innovate – either at school or at work. Simply put, there's a disconnect between the skills the modern business world needs and where training and education budgets have historically been focused.

I wrote this book to fill that gap. I'll walk you through a method for innovating that turns it from something overwhelming and fraught with danger into a series of surprisingly simple steps. A method which makes innovating as predictable and low risk as many of the other tasks you carry out in your job on a daily basis. Yes, really.

Why trust me?

You may be wondering what gives me the right to write a book about innovation. Well, because I've been in your shoes, and succeeded.

One chilly day in November 2011, I arrived at the global headquarters of a leading food and beverage company to undertake a job that, with hindsight, I had no idea how to do. I was to be their Global Innovation Director – a brand new role that had just been created.

On paper, the mission was simple: to help accelerate the growth of an already highly performing, market-leading company through the launch of innovative new products and services. However, the mission was always going to be tough. As my new boss, the CEO, effectively summarized: 'We don't know how to innovate, we know that you don't know how to innovate – but we trust you, so you'll figure it out!'

After an initial period of feeling lost and uncomfortable, I realized there was just one critical part of the puzzle that I was missing. Despite strong success in my career to date, I simply didn't know how to innovate.

So began an exciting and enjoyable mission to test a wide variety of innovation approaches, methods, tools, techniques and tactics, in the real-life context of a leading global corporation. In the process, I identified what worked, as well as the many things that didn't.

The CEO's prediction turned out to be right: I did figure it out. I ended up spending over five years in that role, which turned out to be an exhilarating adventure of getting closer to customers, leading innovation projects, developing new innovation methods, learning from best-in-class innovators, and supporting innovation teams all around the world.

Thankfully it transpired that I was quite good at it, developing several innovations that were not only award-winning but truly helped our customers. What's more, over those five years, innovation became one of the biggest drivers of the company's worldwide growth.

In 2017, I made the decision to leave that job so I could help other businesses to innovate, and founded Innovinco®, the innovation acceleration company. Since then, I've had the privilege of helping over 30 of the world's leading corporations, across almost all industry sectors, to accelerate their innovation performance. And, to achieve this, I've used exactly the same tools and techniques that you'll discover in this book.

Introducing the INNOVATOR Way®

At the heart of this book is the INNOVATOR Way® –
a system born from 15 years of hands-on research
and testing with leading corporations around the
globe. The lessons learned along the way have been
invaluable in understanding why some companies
repeatedly succeed at innovation, and why others
consistently struggle.

This framework guides you through each stage of
the innovation process. It's a robust roadmap which
takes the guesswork out of innovating, making it
much less stressful. It has been deployed in industries
as diverse as cars, construction, healthcare, luxury
and logistics.

It has been trained to business leaders and managers in over 40 countries. Their response has been
overwhelmingly positive, with feedback such as 'perfect roadmap', 'highly valuable', 'easy to understand
and apply' and 'brilliant'. Even more importantly, it
has created some remarkable innovation for their
businesses, with remarkable results.

I intentionally designed the INNOVATOR Way®
as a visual framework which is easy to understand,
practical to use and simple to remember. Compared
with existing innovation frameworks, it brings three
main benefits:

✓ it makes innovating faster, through its action-
oriented approach, and by also capitalizing on
relevant elements of startup methods
✓ it makes innovating more scalable, by providing
a replicable roadmap to follow, which can be
repeated time and time again across a company

✓ it brings confidence, by enabling leaders and managers of all functions to innovate, regardless of previous experience. This is critical: after all, innovating is no longer the responsibility of any one person or department.

The INNOVATOR Way® has 10 steps, which is more than you'll find in most other innovation frameworks. However, believe me, any innovation process that promises results from just three or five stages is over-promising at best. In my experience, it is much more effective to have smaller steps which are shorter, sharper and less overwhelming. It might seem counterintuitive, but smaller steps equal faster progress.

Why is the INNOVATOR Way® so effective?

There are three main reasons for this:

✓ It is a customer-centric approach and can therefore be used to create any type of innovation – products, services or other solutions. This customer-centricity significantly reduces the risk of project failure.
✓ It was created from tried and tested innovation techniques. My objective was never to reinvent the innovation process, but rather to curate, simplify and sharpen a selection of the highest-performing techniques and transform these into a streamlined, end-to-end approach – an approach which is complementary to, not competitive with, a company's existing innovation process.

✓ It covers both hard and so-called 'softer' innovation skills. Innovative projects frequently fail due to 'softer' project issues such as a lack of effective stakeholder management, communication which is not clear or convincing, or a dysfunctional cross-functional team, which is why these elements are also covered.

By including and clarifying all key steps of the end-to-end innovation process, the INNOVATOR Way® significantly increases the probability that innovation will happen, be successful and generate business growth.

How to use this book?

Whilst it may be tempting to dive straight into the 10 steps in Part 2, I recommend that you take the short time required to read Part 1 first. This will ensure that you have a strong foundational understanding of innovation: what it is, and why it's so important. A fragile understanding may cause challenges later on. In Chapter 3, you can assess your starting point as an innovator, which you can revisit later to track your progress over time.

Once you have read the introduction to Part 2, your next steps will depend on whether you're starting a new project or are working on an existing one.

If it's a new innovation project, begin at the first step Fix the Frame in Chapter 4, and then work through the method chapter by chapter, being sure not to miss (or skim too quickly over) any of the steps. If you learn something in one step which challenges your project, or seems like it may derail it, simply go back a step and re-do it before moving forward again. It's completely normal for an innovative project not to be fully linear.

If you're already working on an innovation project, identify what step of the INNOVATOR Way® your project is currently at, and then go back to complete all of the previous steps. This may feel like you're going backwards and wasting time. However, if you don't do this, your project may not be built on solid foundations and therefore have a higher risk of failure.

This is especially important if your innovation project started with a tangible idea for a new product, service or solution (rather than starting with a customer need, pain or desire). Please don't fall into the common and dangerous trap of falling in love with a product, service or solution for which there is no customer need!

I've done my best to keep the language throughout this book as clear and simple as possible, which has been no mean feat! Every time I introduce a new term for the first time, I will mark it in **bold**. A full glossary of terms is included at the end of the book.

Before we begin

INNOVATOR is the book I wish I'd had when I arrived at those corporate headquarters all those years ago. I hope you will find it a powerful and practical playbook which helps you to create bigger, better and faster innovation. I hope that you'll be inspired by the examples from best-in-class innovative companies.

And I hope that it helps you to become an innovation advocate in your organization, and that this leads to a richer and more successful career trajectory.

Fast forwarding to the future for a moment, wouldn't it be great to be seen as an innovator? Someone who understands what innovation is all about? Someone who feels confident about how to innovate, and can inspire and support others with their innovation initiatives? Someone who consistently creates value and delivers growth? Someone who is seen as a future business leader?

I wrote this book because *everyone* has the potential to become a successful innovator. But that won't happen if you don't take action. This is not a book to read passively, but rather an invitation to go and innovate – to make people's lives better, to create some positive change in the world.

Don't aim for perfection immediately. Don't try to do everything at once. Start with one step. Test out a few of the tools and techniques. Start right now, and you'll soon discover your own innovation superpowers.

PART 1:
INNOVATOR FOUNDATIONS

One of the things that I've frequently noticed when working inside large organizations, or helping them from the outside, is that the foundations of innovation understanding are often not strong. And, as we know from the world of construction, weak foundations inevitably lead to weak projects and performance.

And so the first part of this book is dedicated to strengthening your understanding of the fundamentals.

In Chapter 1, we will unpack what innovation is, what it isn't, and how it is different from several similar terms with which it is often associated.

In Chapter 2, we will deep dive into why innovation is so important, and I will share six key reasons why this is the case.

And in Chapter 3, just before we embark on the 10 steps, I will invite you to capture your current level of innovator behaviour, to enable you to see your progress over time.

Let's go!

1

What is innovation?

Everyone talks about innovation – but what is it really?

Whilst the primary focus of this book is on *how* to innovate, before we go any further it's important that we are clear and aligned on *what* innovation is. This is especially important given that *innovation* has become a highly attractive buzzword which is now used frequently and liberally within organizations, and in external communication to customers, shareholders and the media. The word *innovation* has become a bit like the chocolate sauce which is drizzled over a dessert to make it appear more appetizing!

When many people hear the word *innovation*, they spontaneously think of the latest shiny new technology, or visionary Silicon Valley leaders unveiling their new digital gadgets to rapturous applause from the crowd. However, this is not the whole story and, in fact, represents a very limited view, as we will explore below.

There are hundreds of different definitions of the word *innovation*. However, my definition is simply to say that an innovation must demonstrate all three of the following characteristics: new, value and real.

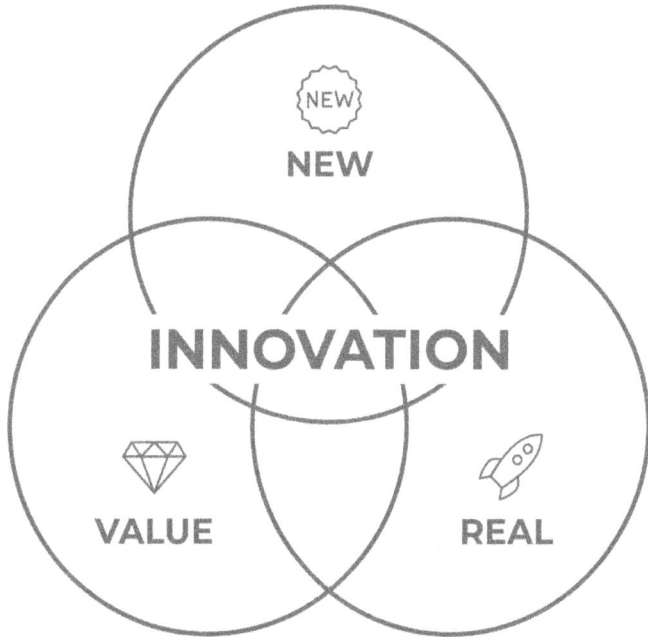

New

Whatever the innovation is, it must contain some element of *new* vs. what exists today: whether that's new to the world, new to a specific country, new to an industry, or new to a company.

Indeed, lots of successful innovation is not completely new to the world, but was inspired by initiatives in other countries, other industries or other companies.

It's important to note that the use of new technology is absolutely not mandatory here; there are many great examples of innovation built on the back of existing or old technologies.

Value

Any innovation must create *value*. In fact, innovation must typically create value for at least two stakeholders:

1. **Customers.** In other words, it must ultimately make some people's lives better in some way. After all, that's all that innovation really is. This may be through bringing positive benefits such as better health, increased wealth and happiness; or indeed through reducing or removing pains, such as frustrations, inefficiencies or inconvenience.

    These customers may be consumers (for **B2C, Business-to-Consumer**) or business customers (for **B2B, Business-to-Business**).

    The value created by an innovation may be life-changing, for example innovation in the pharmaceutical industry. Or the value created might be much less lofty, such as brightening someone's day with an innovative new flavour or format of food or beverage.

2. **Company.** In other words, it must improve the performance of the organization in some way. This is often through generating profitable business growth. But it may be through saving time, money or resources, which also has a direct impact on the bottom line.

If an innovative project only creates value for the customer but not the company, the company is unlikely to support it for very long. If an innovative project only creates value for the company but not the customer, customers are unlikely to support it for very long. In both cases, there will not be a successful innovation performance over time.

Real

An innovation must be *real*. Unless it is tangible and exists in real life, it's not an innovation – because it's not creating value. This means that an innovation must be executable and executed. An innovation is not an idea in someone's head, or a concept written on paper in a drawer somewhere. This is often the key criterion that sets apart highly performing innovative organizations from those that perform less well: the conviction, the grit, the energy, the determination to get innovations launched into the real world.

—

If you accept these three criteria – *new, value, real* – as a definition of innovation, this may challenge some of your preconceived ideas. For example, that innovation must *always* require huge budgets and financial investment. Or that innovation must *always* require a long time to develop and deploy.

Whilst this may be the case depending on the specifics of an innovative project, I strongly discourage you from automatically thinking that this will *always* be the case, as this may kill some highly valuable opportunities before they even get started.

How is innovation different from other similar concepts?

If an innovation must be *new*, create *value* and be *real,* we can use these criteria to determine the differences between other words and concepts that are associated, and often confused, with innovation.

Let's start with ideas. These are a critical ingredient in the innovation process but are not sufficient for innovation success. Ideas often relate to *new*; however they are not yet *real*. Ideas may or may not create *value* for the company or customers – more work is required to determine this and, if relevant, execute them in real life. 'Ideas are cheap and abundant; what is of value is the effective placement of those ideas into situations that develop into action' – a quote often attributed to Peter Drucker, famous business author and educator.

Next, let's think about invention, a word often associated with innovation, partly due to its linguistic similarity. An invention, by definition, must be *new* to the world (after all, the lightbulb can only be invented once), and it must be *real* to be called an invention. However, the *value* for customers or the company has not yet been identified. Sadly, it is common for inventions never to create such value, and for them to only ever achieve gadget status.

Next, technology. Innovation is not the same as technology. Technology is often an enabler for innovation, a means to help make innovation happen, but is not a required ingredient. Technology is often *new* and *real*, but in itself does not create *value*: value is only created when technology successfully helps customers and the company.

Finally, let's think about entrepreneurship. Innovation and entrepreneurship are often bracketed together, especially in the name of business school programmes. However, they are fundamentally different. Entrepreneurship simply means creating a business – whether that business be an innovative startup, or a non-innovative café or barber shop.

So, an entrepreneurial or startup business is *real*, but *new* is not required. Creating *value* is, of course, always the goal; however, unfortunately, there are a high number of entrepreneurial endeavours which do not succeed in achieving this.

What are the different types of innovation?

So now we're clear on what innovation is, let's be more specific about the different types of innovation. Different authors and academics have their own perspectives on how many types of innovation there are, one of the most robust being Larry Keeley et al.'s *Ten Types of Innovation*.

To keep things simple, I consider there to be three broad types:

1. new products
2. new services
3. new solutions

Whilst historically companies were often focused on product-based innovation, there has been an increasing shift in the market towards service-based innovation, often with digitally enabled business models.

For example, in terms of music: whilst we used to own records, cassettes and CDs, today most of us simply stream music from online services such as Spotify. In terms of mobility: there has been an exponential growth in flexible services, with many of us now using ride-hailing companies such as Uber, Lyft, Bolt, Grab,

DiDi, Ola and Gojek. It does not seem that this trend will slow down any time soon, as such service-based innovation can create strong value for both customers and the company.

What do I mean by 'new solutions'? Well, this is a bit of a catch-all for innovation which is not easily classified as a product or service. Innovation can be created wherever a customer has a need, and sometimes it simply doesn't fit neatly under the label of product or service.

The INNOVATOR Way® can be used to create *any* kind of innovation – including process innovation, organizational innovation and innovation in customer experience. In this book, for simplicity, we will view the 10 steps through the lens of product or service innovation. However, please remember that the exact same 10 steps apply whatever kind of innovative solution you would like to create.

From a terminology point of view, from now on I will refer to the output of our innovation method – whether that be a product, service or solution – as an **offer**. This will be our key deliverable upon completing the steps.

—

Actions to accelerate

Here are the top three actions to help you move forward quickly:

1. Schedule a 'What is innovation?' discussion with your leadership team.

2. Use the following **power questions** to help elicit opinions and gain alignment:

> **What is the definition of innovation for our company?**
>
> **Which different types of innovation are the priority for our company – new products, new services or new solutions – and why?**

3. Formalize the outputs in a written one-pager, then share across all key stakeholders.

2

Why is innovation so important?

Senior leaders frequently mention the need for their organizations to innovate. It is a common rallying cry to the troops during town hall meetings, business reviews and team huddles. No one typically disagrees with the sentiment, as innovation is perceived by most people as a no-brainer for organizations to be successful.

However, when asked *why* innovation is so important, people's responses surprisingly often lack precision and alignment.

I realized just how important this was early in my tenure as Global Innovation Director. There was lots of talk in the business about the importance of innovation, inspired by our new CEO, but relatively little action or traction within the business at that stage.

Inspired by Simon Sinek's *Start with Why*, I decided to conduct a small experiment where I asked each of the 10 board members to individually and succinctly articulate why they thought innovation was so critical to the future success of our company.

Interestingly, out of the 10 responses I received, every one of them was different. One mentioned business growth, another mentioned growing market share, another mentioned expanding into new categories, another mentioned capturing new customers, and so on.

None of these responses were wrong – after all, these were all very bright business leaders. However, the lack of explicit alignment in their responses demonstrated a lack of clarity about the role that innovation needed to play in moving the company strategy forward.

No surprise then that innovation was struggling to secure traction within the organization without clarity on this fundamental *why*.

Whatever the specific reason may be for a company to need to innovate, I believe that there are six underlying reasons why all companies need to do so, including yours:

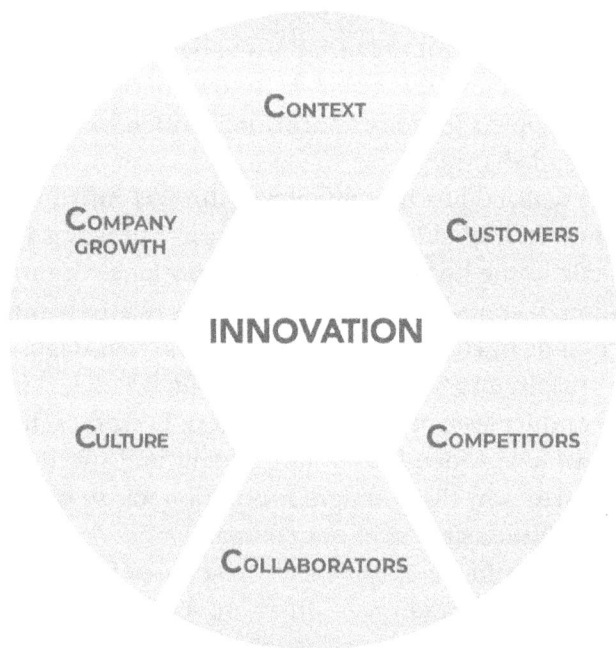

CONTEXT

COMPANY
GROWTH

CUSTOMERS

INNOVATION

CULTURE

COMPETITORS

COLLABORATORS

Context

Innovation increases your company's ability to react positively to changes in its context. The context in which any company exists is in a constant state of flux, whether that's political, economic, social, technological, environmental or legal. And given recent advances in technologies such as artificial intelligence and quantum computing, the rate of change is only going to accelerate over time.

Innovation acts as the bridge between where your company is now and how it will succeed in tomorrow's world. It will not only help your company to survive, but also to thrive by adapting to, and profiting from, these changes in context.

Customers

Innovation increases your value to customers. Remember that the *raison d'être* for companies is to serve customer needs – in a profitable way for the company, of course. However, customer needs evolve and change over time.

So, if your company doesn't evolve at the same pace, you're likely to lose value, relevance and desirability in your customers' world. This is especially important in today's social media culture where people are constantly looking for their fix of new. If your company is not providing new news through innovation, unfortunately it can quickly become old news.

Competitors

Innovation increases your competitive advantage. Unfortunately, your company doesn't exist in a vacuum; it exists within a broad landscape of businesses who are also pushing products, services and solutions to your customers. With increasing globalization, rapidly changing markets and the continued rise of startups, there have never been more businesses competing for your customers' attention and wallet.

Innovating is therefore critical to stay ahead of the pack, to remain your customers' most obvious choice. Remember that your competitors are also trying to serve customer needs better every day through innovation. So, unless you innovate continually, your company is likely to get left behind or, worse still, die.

Collaborators

Innovation increases your attractiveness to collaborators. Here, I'm not talking about colleagues or fellow employees, but rather potential business partners.

Success in today's business world is increasingly coming from forging win-win partnerships and alliances with external organizations who bring complementary brands, assets, skills or capability. Innovating helps to attract potential partners and capitalize on collaborative growth opportunities. No one wants to partner with a dinosaur organization that is not looking to the future.

Culture

Innovation increases the strength of your company culture. One of the things that I've consistently observed over the years is the power of innovation to create positive energy and motivation within a company. Innovation gets people excited, aligned, and boosts their pride in working for the organization, due to its inherent positivity.

This cultural aspect should not be underestimated when it comes to talent acquisition. Potential recruits want to know that the company is future-facing and dynamic, to feel confident in their decision to join.

Company growth

Most importantly of all, innovation can significantly increase your company growth. Innovation can influence your existing customers to buy more, buy more often and pay more. Innovation can also help you to recruit new customers, which clearly also brings business growth.

Whilst the idea of businesses always needing to grow is sometimes challenged, especially in the context of sustainability and corporate social responsibility, I believe that it must remain a critical business objective. Growth brings the financial resources required to secure a company's future, as well as the financial freedom to create positive social impact.

—

So those are my six underlying reasons why innovation is so critical for any company. It's not just about enabling your business to survive today but also preparing for it to thrive into the future.

Innovation in the service of strategy

One important point before we close this chapter. Despite its importance, we must remember that innovation is always a means to achieve something, not an endgame in itself. That something should be strategy. All innovation efforts and projects should be dedicated to advancing the overall company strategy; i.e. the fully thought-through, fully aligned plan which outlines its goals and priorities for success.

This alignment with strategy leads to a much greater impact from innovation. It also maximizes the probability that you get the resources and budget you need to succeed with your innovation project, and that these are less likely to be cut in case of trickier times.

Surprisingly this alignment is not always the case: it is common to see innovation teams and projects floating in their own bubble – exemplified by personal pet projects, innovation theatre and low levels of accountability. The good news is that this is easy to fix, as we will see in Chapter 4.

—

Actions to accelerate

Here are the top three actions to help you move forward quickly:

1. Schedule a 'Why is innovation important for us?' discussion with your leadership team.
2. Use the following power questions to help elicit opinions and gain alignment:

Why is innovation important for the success of our company?

How can innovation help to move our strategy forward?

Why is it important to accelerate our innovation efforts now?

What will happen to our company if we don't innovate?

You may also want to replicate the experiment I mentioned above, by getting individual responses from the participants before the session, which can act as stimulus for discussion and also highlight the need for alignment.

3. Formalize the outputs in a written one-pager, then share with all key stakeholders.

3

Where are you starting from?

Whilst I know that you are probably itching to get cracking with the 10 steps, I'd like to invite you to capture your starting point. Not your starting point in terms of an innovation project, but rather your starting point as an innovator today.

Very often, especially within large organizations, we spend a lot of time thinking about our jobs, our objectives, our projects and our teams. But, for a short moment, I want you to think about yourself, and where *you* currently are on *your* innovator journey.

Why is this important? Well, getting an understanding of your current level of innovation expertise will help you understand how easy or challenging you may find it to innovate successfully today. And it will also be motivating to see your progress over time.

That's why I've developed the INNOVATOR Scorecard as a companion tool for readers of this book. It is a short online questionnaire, which captures the degree to which you demonstrate the core behaviours of successful innovators.

When you've finished, you will receive a personalized report from me via email. This is completely free of charge, a gift to thank you for buying this book.

This report will help you understand where your innovator strengths are today, as well as potential blind spots. It will help you as you work through the chapters which follow, to determine on which steps it will be important for you to put the most focus.

Whatever your scores, please remember that this is just a tool to capture a snapshot of where you are today. Reading the rest of this book is already a great way to quickly boost your innovator performance!

—

Actions to accelerate

Here are the top three actions to help you move forward quickly:

1. Head over to the INNOVATOR Scorecard right now by either flashing the QR code below, or by going to **InnovatorScorecard.com**
2. Complete the questionnaire. This is simple and will only take a few minutes.
3. Read your report, making a mental note of the key areas to focus on.

PART 2:

INNOVATOR WAY

Before we dive into the details of each of the 10 steps, I thought it might be helpful to quickly share a brief overview of the INNOVATOR Way® framework and also answer a few frequently asked questions.

Overview of the INNOVATOR Way®

Let's go through the 10 steps one by one:

Step 1: Fix the Frame

This first step is a preliminary step. It helps you to ensure that your project is fully connected to company strategy, that the key parameters of your project are clear and aligned, and that the way to move the project forward is agreed. This step is graphically represented by the two framing brackets in the visual on the previous page.

The remaining nine steps take place within this agreed **frame**. They have been designed to be easy to remember, thanks to the INNOVATOR acronym and the alliterative names. This memorability helps drive actionability.

Furthermore, the colour of each step has been specifically chosen to represent the activities, behaviours and emotions at that step. Have a quick look at the visual on the front cover of this book before reading on, or alternatively at **InnovatorBook.com**

Step 2: Immerse and Inquire

This step is all about gathering **customer clues** and getting out of the office to interact directly with customers. We will use these customer clues to build a strong, relevant and valuable innovation project.

This is 'the red step': red being the colour most associated with strength and courage, as well as warmth and love – perfect ingredients for successful interactions with customers.

Step 3: Narrow the Need

This step is all about digesting, connecting and prioritizing the customer clues you have gathered, and then crafting a powerful insight on which you will build your innovation project.

This is 'the dark orange step', as orange is connected to high levels of curiosity – exactly what's required at this stage.

Step 4: Nail a Northstar

This step is all about setting a bold ambition in the way that you define your innovation brief, such that the ideas that you will create will also be as ambitious as possible.

This is 'the light orange step', as orange is also perceived as the colour of confidence, which is exactly what you need here.

Step 5: Open up Options

This step is all about generating as many relevant and innovative ideas as possible, prioritizing the strongest one, and then articulating it in a precise way.

This is 'the yellow step', as yellow is the colour which evokes creativity, new ideas, optimism, freshness and playfulness – all of which are critical here.

Step 6: Verify the Value

This step is all about prototyping your idea, getting it in front of customers as quickly as possible, and refining it based on their feedback. This is an iterative step, meaning that you do it as many times as necessary, until you have sufficient confidence to launch.

This is 'the green step', with green often used to denote 'go', show a positive result or the right path to follow – perfectly aligned with what we're trying to achieve here.

Step 7: Achieve the Ambition

This step is all about turning your innovation project into reality, making it easy for your customers to buy your offer, and getting them excited to buy.

This is 'the light blue step', given that blue is the colour of trust, relationships, loyalty and commitments, which is exactly what we're aiming for from our customers.

Step 8: Track the Traction

This step is all about proactively understanding how your offer is performing post-launch, by compiling and analysing data, and drawing conclusions.

This is 'the dark blue step', as blue is also the colour of clarity, credibility, efficiency, reliability and precision, all of which are required to do this step effectively.

Step 9: Optimize the Offer

This step is all about exploring different options to improve the performance of your offer, based on conclusions from the previous step, before deciding what you are going to implement and when.

This is 'the light purple step', given that purple is the colour of transformation towards excellence and superior quality, fully aligned with our objective here.

Step 10: Reflect and Review

This step is all about taking a step back at the end of the project to think about what went well, less well, and what should be changed for future projects to ensure improved innovation performance over time.

This is the 'dark purple step', as purple is also the colour of wisdom, deeper understanding and knowledge, which is exactly what we are looking for at this final step.

—

Verify the Value

As you can see in the main visual, the Verify the Value 'V' step sits at the heart of the INNOVATOR Way®. This is not by chance, but by design, as it represents one of the central philosophies of the methodology: that it is critical to check with your customers that your project is moving in a robust and relevant direction.

Whilst Verify the Value has its own specific step, it is centrally positioned within the framework as customer check-ins should ideally also be done during the other steps too. This iterative 'looping back' with customers throughout the process, popularized by innovation methods such as Design Thinking, is one of the most powerful ways to reduce the level of risk on your project, thereby maximizing your probability of success.

Sub-steps

To further help you to put the INNOVATOR Way® into action, I have divided each of the 10 steps into three more granular sub-steps. This will help you to be clear on what you specifically need to do next to move forward. Overleaf is the complete overview of the INNOVATOR Way®, with steps and sub-steps:

FIX THE FRAME — WHY? · WHO? · WHAT? · WHERE? · WHEN? · HOW?

I — IMMERSE AND INQUIRE — LISTEN · OBSERVE · QUESTION

N — NARROW THE NEED — COLLATE · CONNECT · CRAFT

N — NAIL A NORTHSTAR — ASPIRE · BENCHMARK · CHOOSE

O — OPEN UP OPTIONS — DIVERGE · CONVERGE · SPECIFY

V — VERIFY THE VALUE — PROTOTYPE · TEST · IMPROVE

A — ACHIEVE THE AMBITION — ACCESS · ACTIVATE · ACTUALIZE

T — TRACK THE TRACTION — COMPILE · ANALYSE · CONCLUDE

O — OPTIMIZE THE OFFER — EXPLORE · PRIORITIZE · IMPLEMENT

R — REFLECT AND REVIEW — CELEBRATE · CRITIQUE · CALIBRATE

Power questions

The INNOVATOR Way® capitalizes on power questions. For many years I was convinced that the focus of innovation was on finding answers; however, I have subsequently learned that asking the right questions is significantly more important and leads to much stronger results. Great innovators ask great questions.

You will find power questions at every step. They will help you to frame your innovation project, better understand customer needs, be more ambitious with your idea generation, test your idea, launch your offer with success, and capture learnings for future projects. Power questions will also help you to engage other people with your project and get their inputs and support.

To get the maximum benefit from these power questions, don't just ask them to yourself, but also to relevant stakeholders, colleagues and members of your project team. This will ensure that your answers are stronger, richer and more aligned.

Timeframe

Unlike some innovation methods, there is no defined timeframe attached to the INNOVATOR Way®. This is because projects are different, companies are different and industries are different.

However, one quick comment. When I work with large companies and ask them how long it takes to develop and launch an innovation project, the spontaneous response, almost without thinking, is often '18 months'; 18 months is often the time it takes them today, using their current process, linked with their budget cycle or business calendar.

For complex innovation projects, or those requiring an innovative technology, 18 months may seem very short, and may be unrealistic. It may take longer, even much longer.

However, for innovation projects which are less complex or don't require new innovative technology, the INNOVATOR Way® does not need to take 18 months – it can be done in a much more accelerated way, especially Steps 1 to 6 which are focused on the development of the innovation offer.

My advice? Try to push yourselves to progress more quickly than you feel comfortable with, as this urgency and feeling that you're on an exciting short-term mission can bring a helpful boost of energy and ensure that your project doesn't lose momentum.

What if I get stuck?

As I mentioned briefly in the Introduction, if you learn something at one step which challenges your project, or seems like it may derail it, I recommend to go back a step and re-do that step, before moving forward again. Innovation projects are rarely completely linear: they often require some level of iterating, reworking and retesting.

Obviously, I cannot provide a one-size-fits-all piece of advice which is guaranteed to unstick your project, but the closest I can get is this: if in doubt, go back to your customers. Either the customer clues that you will have already gathered or go back to meet with them in person. Let their inputs guide your next steps.

Ultimately, to succeed with your innovative project, you will need your customers to buy, use or consume your offer, and therefore some additional input from them can be invaluable to help get your project moving forward again in the right direction.

Without further ado, let's get cracking with Step 1, Fix the Frame.

4

Step 1: Fix the Frame

'But how does this innovation project move the company strategy forward?'

A seemingly simple and innocuous question, but one to which no answer was forthcoming from the increasingly embarrassed innovation project leader. After a few moments, the silence became deafening. And after a short follow-up conversation, it transpired that her project wasn't actually going to move the company strategy forward at all...

This exchange, heard many times during my career, perfectly illustrates one of the most curious, but very widespread, phenomena in innovation. I call it 'innovating without intent': embarking on a journey to innovate, without being fully clear on where you're going or why. Can you imagine an architect who starts to build a house without first being clear on where to build it and why they're building it in the first place? Unsurprisingly, this approach rarely results in innovation success.

'But we would never do that, we are too smart!', I hear you cry. Whilst this may be true, data suggests you would be in the minority. According to recent research from BCG (Manly et al., 2024), just 12% of companies report a strong link between strategy and innovation. Yes, just 12%. So why does this happen? In my experience, there are two primary causes:

1. Company strategy is often not sharp enough

In the aforementioned BCG research, the top challenge cited by companies regarding innovation/R&D/product development is 'unclear or overly broad strategy'.

At some point over the past 20 years, we have confused the painful annual business planning ritual of writing a 232-page PowerPoint deck with that of having a clear, sharp and solid company strategy. We have forgotten that the true meaning of the word 'strategy' is that of 'a plan of action', rather than slides of lofty analysis.

Grossly paraphrasing Blaise Pascal, the French mathematician and philosopher, company strategies are only written long-hand because we don't take the time or make the effort to write them in a short and simple way. In my career, the most effective business strategies have been able to be summarized onto the side of a mug – which incidentally, as a highly visible object on a team member's desk, can also help drive daily implementation!

A strong strategy is one which simply defines how the company will win in its market, in a profitable way, with clarity on what makes it different and better than competitors. A strong strategy also explicitly says 'no' to enable focus on what truly matters.

2. Innovation is led by humans, not robots

Even in today's world increasingly powered by artificial intelligence and algorithms, innovators are humans rather than robots. Despite best efforts, we are naturally drawn towards what we like, what excites us and what motivates us. This easily leads to 'pet projects': innovation projects with which we fall in love on a personal level, regardless of their level of connection to company strategy.

An alternative manifestation of this is 'trophy projects': where we perceive the projects as so high profile and overwhelmingly attractive that we prioritize them, consciously or subconsciously, to achieve personal recognition and glory – again regardless of their level of direct connection to company strategy.

Trophy projects are particularly prevalent when innovating through the acquisition of smaller companies or startups. After all, being at the head of such a high-profile acquisition initiative is almost universally perceived as positive both inside and outside of an organization, regardless of whether any business results have yet been delivered. Trophy projects are often stepping stones to assuring future promotion.

—

Simply put, the goal of this preliminary Fix the Frame step is to ensure that, *before* you actively start working on an innovation project, there is a direct and inextricable link between what you are going to work on and the agreed company strategy; i.e. that the project will proactively move the company towards where it has decided it needs to go to be successful.

At this step, you also paint the picture of what success on the project looks like. In the words of Steven Covey of *7 Habits* fame, we 'begin with the end in mind'. You must have a clear vision of your desired destination. This does not mean the final offer itself (at this first step of the project, you obviously have no idea what this will be), but rather the positive impact you want it to have on your business.

Whilst I am the first person to want to get stuck into starting an innovation project, this preliminary step is fundamental to maximizing the probability of project success. Especially given that BCG's research also demonstrates that companies with a strong link between strategy and innovation achieve a share of revenue from new products that is 74% higher than companies with a weak link.

So let's go!

—

Objective

The objective of this preliminary Fix the Frame step is to clearly articulate and align on the parameters within which you want to innovate. This frame is a prerequisite which needs to be in place before starting to move any innovation project forward and will act as the 'guardrails' throughout the life of the project.

Why is this step so important?

There are four key reasons why this step is so important:

✓ It ensures a strong and explicit connection between your innovation project and the wider company strategy and business goals. As well as the aforementioned benefits of this, there are also significant secondary benefits. These include greater ease of securing human and financial resources to move your project forward, and a reduced risk of project deprioritization in the case of a tougher business or economic climate.

✓ This step forces you to be customer-centric, by getting you to identify who you are trying to help through your innovation project from the get-go and getting you to articulate what customer impact you are ideally looking to achieve. This maximizes the probability that your innovation project will indeed create value for customers.

✓ It allows you to focus your time and energy, by defining the project's 'where to play' boundaries.

Your frame will enable you to be clear on what is in project scope and, almost as importantly, what is outside of project scope – as otherwise these elements can be unhelpful distractions as you move through the project.

✓ This step facilitates speed and efficiency in decision-making. Formalizing the frame of your project, and formal validation of this frame from all key stakeholders prior to the start of the project, guarantees a stronger alignment on the scope and the fact that this is a project worth pursuing. As long as your project continues to operate within the agreed and aligned frame, the project team can typically enjoy more autonomy and empowerment, with less micro-management and interference.

What are the key risks if we skip this step or do it badly?

There are two key risks:

- Despite your great efforts, you may end up with a project which is ultimately not supported by your company, or not wanted by your customers. Or a project which is off-strategy, or simply too small in scale vs. strategic goals.

  Clearly this leads to the undesirable situation of wasting company time and money, as well as your time and energy and that of the project team. This can ultimately lead to a negative impact on both company performance and reputation.

- Without the level of focus that this project frame provides, it is likely that your innovation efforts and resources will be spread too thinly, thereby leading to low or no positive impact for your company or your customers.

  As company resources and employee time are largely fixed, it is unsurprisingly more effective to make clear choices about where to innovate, rather than attempting the impossible of successfully innovating all things for all people.

Steps to success

The Fix the Frame step is surprisingly simple, but incredibly powerful. Your task will be to articulate and align on answers to the six 'W' questions which make up the six sub-steps below – WHY? WHO? WHAT? WHERE? WHEN? and HOW?

WHY?	WHO?	WHAT?	WHERE?	WHEN?	HOW?

In the pages that follow, we'll work through each of these one by one.

The answers to these six questions, when summarized, will create a clear frame for your project. At the end of this step, the format of your frame will look something like this:

Through this innovation project,
we want to accelerate business growth by **A%**
by **B** timings [WHY]
by getting our core customers who are **C**,
and who think/feel/do **D, E** and **F** [WHO]
to increase their [growth goal]
from **G** to **H**
by delighting them with a new offer related to **I**
[strategic scope]
which they will purchase/use/consume at **J** and **K**
[WHERE & WHEN]

We will progress this project by
assembling **Z** [taskforce team]
who will spend **Y** amount of time until **X** date
[time commitment]
with this support [required resources]

For decision-making and to manage
key stakeholders, we commit to
update [stakeholders]
via [meeting instance or
communication channel]
every [update frequency]

WHY?

The very first question to ask is WHY? as a means of identifying the overarching goal behind your innovation project. Whilst this may seem like a simple and obvious question to ask, I estimate that the majority of innovation project leaders I've met over the years have been unable to give an immediate, clear or concise response regarding why their project exists.

To help you formalize your answer to this, here are two initial power questions:

> **Why is this innovation project important to move our strategy forward?**

> **Why should our company prioritize this project?**

In this sub-step, it is also important to draft the business objectives for the innovation project. In many cases, this will be a business growth objective that is linked to wider company strategy. It may feel quite early for you to start to think about this. However, remember that innovation projects are 'only' means to achieving business objectives. And the size and scale of the business objective will have a fundamental impact on the size and scale of the innovation project. Here are two simple power questions:

> **What do we want this innovation project to achieve from a business perspective?**

> **And by when?**

The 'by when' element of this power question is important. The time horizon by which you are looking to launch your new offer is likely to influence the level of disruption and also the type of technology you may potentially use.

An innovative offer which you only have six months to develop and launch may not be the same as an offer to be launched in three years' time. (As an aside, it can sometimes be very powerful to deliberately shrink project timings, as you will find you make faster and more efficient progress if you need to operate under such a time constraint.)

These timings will help you to create a project plan, and also prioritize between different projects, to ensure that you deliver on time vs. stakeholder expectations.

WHO?

The second question to ask is WHO? as a way of defining the customer profile you want to help via your innovation project. As previously mentioned, customer-centricity is the key success factor for innovation, meaning that you should ideally be clear from the start about which customer profile you are focusing on, to enable you to develop solutions which are highly relevant.

Here are two power questions you can use to help with this:

> **Who is our core customer for this innovation project, and why?**

**Who do we want to help most through
our innovation project?**

We will continue to use the term **core customer** throughout this book. The word 'core' is important here: there are likely to be many different customer profiles who ultimately buy, use or consume your innovative offer. However, you are more likely to succeed by focusing your innovation efforts on a 'core' customer profile.

This may seem counterintuitive, as surely you will sell more if you try to appeal to a larger pool of customers, right? Well, no. The more specific you are in sharply identifying a group of core customers, the more deeply you will understand the specific needs of that group, and therefore the higher the probability that you will create an offer that truly delivers value for them – and also delivers greater value to them than competitor offers.

The customer power questions just above can be further broken down into the following two additional power questions:

**Who is the beneficiary who will use or consume
our new offer?**

**Who is the buyer who will buy or pay for
our new offer?**

The **beneficiary** is sometimes referred to as the 'end-user'. However, I am not a huge fan of this term, especially as the verb 'use' is not naturally used in conjunction with many products, services or solutions. After all, when did you last 'use' cakes or champagne, 'use' your bank or insurance, or 'use' a hotel or restaurant?

I much prefer the term beneficiary; i.e. the person who will ultimately benefit from your innovative offer. This word also serves as a useful reminder that an innovative offer must indeed bring benefits!

The answer to the above two power questions may be the same; i.e. the **buyer** and the beneficiary are the same person. For example, someone who buys a car is often also the person who benefits from it. However, this is sometimes not the case.

Think for a moment about baby food. The beneficiary is the baby, whereas the buyer is the parent or guardian. An innovative project in baby food can therefore only be successful if you satisfy the needs and desires of *both* buyer and beneficiary.

This is also often the case in B2B. Think for a moment about office supplies. The beneficiaries are the employees who use the paper, pens, staplers, notebooks, etc., whereas the buyer is likely to be the office manager.

An innovation project can only be successful if you satisfy the needs and desires of both groups of core customers – beneficiaries and buyers – meaning that we must identify these from the very beginning of the project, in this initial Fix the Frame step.

Whilst you will learn much more about your core customers in Step 2, Immerse and Inquire, capture any key characteristics you already know about them here in your frame. You can use the following power questions to help with this:

**What are the profiles of the core customers
for our new offer?**

Which attributes can we use to define them?

What do our core customers think, feel and do?

It is important to be as specific as possible whenever we describe core customers. Whilst it can be tempting to only capture demographic details (for example, age, sex, income), it is critical to also capture customers' key attitudes and behaviours, as these can have a significant impact on their wants and needs, and therefore their usage, consumption and purchase behaviour.

Before you finish this sub-step, use the following power questions to maximize the probability that your project will deliver the desired results:

**Are the beneficiary and buyer for our
innovation project 100% aligned and consistent
with company strategy?**

**Are they significant enough in terms of size and
purchasing power [i.e. ability to pay] to drive a
sufficiently significant level of business growth?**

WHAT?

The third question to ask is WHAT? This doesn't mean that you should already know the specifics of the offer that you will ultimately launch, as clearly it is far too early for that!

There are two key elements to define at this sub-step: the **growth goal** and the **strategic scope**.

Let's start with two power questions to help define your growth goal:

> **What do we want our core customers to do differently as a result of us launching our new offer?**
>
> **What is our primary growth goal for this project, and by how much do we want to increase it?**

Growth goals are the way in which you want to influence your core customers' behaviour through this innovation project, compared with their behaviour towards your company, brand or products today. Do you want:

⇒ **your existing customers to BUY MORE?**
   i.e. increase their quantity
⇒ **your existing customers to buy MORE OFTEN?**
   i.e. increase their frequency
⇒ **your existing customers to PAY MORE?**
   i.e. increase their value through higher pricing
⇒ **MORE CUSTOMERS to buy from you?**
   i.e. recruit new customers

Here is a visual summary of these four possible growth goals:

| BUY MORE | MORE OFTEN | PAY MORE | MORE CUSTOMERS |

Innovation can help you achieve all four of the growth goals above. However, it is critical to identify which growth goal is the *most* important: an offer designed to recruit new customers is likely to be very different to an offer designed to get your existing customers to buy more often, for example. The growth goal you choose will strongly determine the type of offer you will create.

For your industry, company or strategy, some of the above four growth goals may not be relevant or appropriate. For example, it may not be an appropriate objective to try to get customers to purchase more or more often from your company for sustainability reasons. This isn't a problem – you simply need to focus on the growth goal that *is* most relevant and appropriate.

Moving onto strategic scope. The key power question here is:

Is there a specific scope which has already been identified for our new innovative offer as part of the company strategy?

Examples of strategic scope could be:

- a specific customer need that you are not currently serving well
- a specific product category or format for which you don't currently have an offer
- a specific new type of service which may bring additional revenue
- a specific trend that has been identified as relevant for your business.

If such a strategic scope has already been identified, capture it here, and pressure-check it using the following power questions:

Is the strategic scope substantial enough to drive a sufficiently significant level of business growth?

Is the strategic scope truly 100% aligned and consistent with company strategy?

If no strategic scope has been identified at this stage, there is absolutely no problem: it can be left wide open at this stage, and the direction of your innovation project will be directly guided by what you will learn from your core customers in subsequent steps.

WHERE?

The fourth question to ask is WHERE? Knowing where your offer will ultimately be purchased, used or consumed will help you to ensure that it truly responds to the needs of core customers in those places. It will help you to capitalize on the opportunities these places may bring, as well as respect any specific constraints.

At a macro-level, the WHERE needs to include the geography or geographies where you think your innovative offer may ultimately be launched – as customers in different countries can clearly have very different attitudes, behaviours and needs.

At a micro-level, the WHERE is likely to be different for the buyer and the beneficiary. For example, the buyer may purchase your offer in a retail or online store, whereas this is rarely the point of use or consumption for the beneficiary.

Some power questions to help with this:

**What is the geographical scope
of our new offer?**
i.e. will our new offer be destined for specific
continents, countries, regions or cities?

What is the channel scope for our new offer?
i.e. in which types of distribution channels do
we intend for our new offer to be purchased?
Hypermarkets? Convenience stores?
E-commerce?

**Where do we intend our new offer
to be used or consumed?**
In the home? Out of the home? On the go?

It doesn't matter if you don't have a clear view of these elements yet. The important thing is to capture and formalize them if you, or your stakeholders, do.

WHEN?

The fifth question to ask is WHEN? Knowing when your offer will ultimately be purchased, used or consumed will help ensure that it truly responds to the needs of core customers at those times. It will help you to capitalize on the opportunities those moments may bring, as well as respect any specific constraints.

For your core customers, there may be a specific season, month, occasion, day of the week, or time of day when their need for your new offer will be greater. Or timing may be triggered by certain needs, life events or special occasions.

Timings may well differ between the buyer who will purchase and the beneficiary who will use or consume it. So the two key power questions here are:

**When do we intend our new offer
to be purchased?**
Winter or Summer? Weekdays or weekends?
Morning or evening? Just before a baby is born?

**When do we intend our new offer
to be used or consumed?**
During breakfast? Whilst working?
After sport? During social gatherings?

Again, if this is not yet clear for your project, no problem. The important thing is to capture and formalize these timings if you, or your stakeholders, are already aware of them.

HOW?

Clearly any innovation project needs a plan to concretely move it forward, and it is at this HOW sub-step that this is identified.

Let's work through these elements one by one.

Starting with team. My preferred wording here is **taskforce team**, as I've found that this brings a greater sense of shared mission and energy than the more bland 'project team'. This wording is especially helpful in companies where project teams are not allocated until project approval is granted, and where no project can be approved until the offer is defined, which clearly requires the work of a team. A classic catch-22!

Whilst the impetus for an innovation project often comes from an individual, developing and delivering successful innovation is definitely a team sport, which benefits from a variety of cross-disciplinary backgrounds and skills. Avoid the temptation to only recruit team members that you already know or like. The diversity of backgrounds brings a diversity of perspectives which will make your offer stronger.

Set your sights as high as possible on potential taskforce team members by using the following power question:

> **Who is most likely to help us deliver the most successful result on our project?**

Try to avoid a situation where your taskforce team consists of people who happen to be available. It can be useful to remember that in the startup world, the team is evaluated by venture capitalists as being even more important than their business idea! Don't forget that you can also integrate relevant external partners from outside your company into your taskforce team, where this brings complementary expertise or capability.

Regarding time commitment. In an ideal world, your taskforce team will be fully dedicated to your innovation project as their number one and only priority, as this will drive the fastest and most efficient project progress. This avoids the common undesirable situation where members of the team are repeatedly dragged back to work on operational day-to-day priorities.

A part-time team approach can still work, providing that there is sufficient discipline and alignment around how much time each taskforce team member will spend, and how and when team members will collaborate and communicate. The other condition is that these are the *right* people, by which I mean committed, passionate team players, who bring the expertise required for project success.

If possible, look for what I call **innovator energy**. Not only will your taskforce team need energy to get your project started (often from scratch) and keep it going (especially when challenges inevitably arrive along the way), but they are also going to need contagious energy to enthuse other people about your project with as much passion as you have. Key characteristics of innovator energy are positivity, optimism, dynamism, proactivity and agility.

Let's now move on to resources or, as I prefer to refer to them, **required resources**. This wording is helpful because it encourages you to think about what's truly required (i.e. without which the project cannot proceed), vs. those resources which are nice-to-have, but not critical.

This is where budget comes in. Whilst lack of budget is often cited as a barrier for not innovating, this is often an excuse: the early stages of an innovation project can often be undertaken with very little money. Having limited budget can actually boost powerful innovator behaviours that we will see later in this book, such as going to talk to customers directly, low-resolution prototyping, and test and learn experimentation.

Having said that, it is important that there is *some* budget formally allocated to an innovation project, for two key reasons.

First, as budget allocation is typically aligned with company priorities, receiving budget for an innovative project is an explicit signal that your project is perceived as important. Conversely, if the company is not prepared to put any budget behind a project, it is unlikely that they perceive it as truly important. Second, having easy access to some budget allows your project to move forward more quickly and efficiently, as you don't require approval for every single spend.

Use the following power question to help with this:

**What are the resources we require
without which we are not confident
of success on this project?**

Finally, let's think about **stakeholder strategy**. Stakeholders have the power to make or break your innovation project, and therefore it's important to define a specific strategy for proactively managing them to reduce risk. The power questions here are:

> **Which stakeholders have a decision-making role in our project or can influence it in a significant way?**
>
> **How are we going to update them and how often?**

The means here is important – your project may progress in quite a different way if your stakeholder strategy is based on updating them at a formal quarterly meeting vs. via a more immediate communication channel like email, for example.

Make sure to explicitly agree this with these individuals to ensure that there is full alignment on expectations from the start, including update frequency, and make sure to reconfirm alignment if stakeholders change during the life of the project.

—

This Fix the Frame step may appear quite heavy and will take some time and effort. However, if you do it, you will gain significantly more time and speed during the rest of the project.

As I've already mentioned, it is normal that you might not have all of these elements at this stage. The key is simply to identify and capture as many of these elements as you have so far.

You will have lots of notes and reflections from these six sub-steps. Before moving on, try to summarize these in the frame format shown at the beginning of this chapter. Here's a fictional example:

**Through this innovation project,
we want to accelerate business growth by 5%
over the next 3 years
by getting our Conscious Champion customers
who are passionate about
health, fitness and the environment
to increase their purchase frequency
from 1x per month to 2x per month
by delighting them with a new food offer
which they will purchase in supermarkets
and consume at home**

**We will progress this project by
assembling a taskforce team of
Alex, Bob, Carrie, Daisy and Ed
who will spend 50% of their time
for the next 18 months
with an initial budget of €50,000
and a dedicated project room**

**For decision-making and to manage
key stakeholders, we commit to
present an update to the Innovation Committee
during their bimonthly meetings**

Top tips

✓ Fixing the Frame is not a one-person task. No one can answer all these questions by themselves – so make sure to capitalize on the collective intelligence of colleagues, your taskforce team and other relevant stakeholders.

✓ Make sure that your frame feels fresh; i.e. not just a copy and paste rehash of previous projects, especially if these were not successful or became highly political.

✓ Try to ensure that your frame is interesting and inherently attractive for your stakeholders and also your taskforce team. Put yourself in their shoes and ask 'Would this frame inspire me to want to work on this?'

✓ Check that it is practical and realistic for your taskforce team to meet with, observe and interview the core customer profile you have selected in your frame, as otherwise this will create challenges later on.

✓ Ideally also formally capture what's *outside* the frame; i.e. things that are explicitly *excluded* from project scope. This creates greater clarity for the taskforce team and avoids wasting time and energy on directions which the company has already decided that it does not want to pursue or are not relevant. This will also enable you to push back and say 'no' if stakeholders start to suggest 'scope creep'.

Lessons from leaders

Google undertakes rigorous project framing. We can see this in how they prepare for one of their famous 5-day Design Sprints, an approach pioneered at Google Ventures, where clear scope and structure at the beginning are critical success factors.

Their initial framing articulates the project's goal and deliverables, aligns the team and stakeholders, and clarifies the how. Four of the key elements are defining the challenge, target, team and timeframe:

Challenge. Their process begins with an exercise called 'Start at the End' which lays out the long-term goal for the project. Participants are invited to imagine what will have improved in their business as a result of the project, defining clear success metrics upfront.

They advise to systematically go after a really big and important challenge with high stakes. Just like innovation projects, sprints require a lot of energy and focus, and people simply won't bring their best efforts for something that's small or nice-to-have. I give the exact same advice before undertaking any project with the INNOVATOR Way®.

Google also recommends formally reviewing and aligning on the challenge with leadership during the initial planning stages to ensure that the solutions generated will have the necessary support to be implemented at the end of the project.

Target. Who is the target customer?

Team. Google also advocates for bringing together a cross-functional group of people, including profiles representing Marketing and Customer, Finance, Tech/Logistics and Design. This group should include the people who will ultimately be responsible for executing the solution.

Decisions here also include identifying the 'Decider', as well as how and when they are going to be involved. They also recommend a Facilitator role who is responsible for leading the process, who is ideally unbiased about the decisions, and keeps everything on track – much like a project manager.

Timeframe. What timeframe are we looking at for this project?

Whilst this Design Sprint approach was originally developed at Google, it has been subsequently deployed with success at many companies, such as Slack, Nest and Medium.

Actions to accelerate

Here are the top three actions to help you move forward quickly:

1. Block some time in your diary, with relevant colleagues or your taskforce team, to work through each of the six sub-steps, to draft your frame.
2. Facilitate this session using the power questions, making it as engaging as possible. Ideally you will do this session in person rather than online, in which case you can have a poster on the wall for each of the six sub-steps and get participants to share their thoughts using sticky notes.

3. During this session, capture the inputs of each participant by getting them to work individually at first. This makes sure that everyone's input is captured (not just the loudest or most senior people in the room) and that diverse thoughts are also captured and discussed.

5

Step 2:
Immerse and Inquire

Back when I was working as a Global Innovation Director, we had fixed the frame on an Older Adults core customer profile as a potential source of business growth through innovation: an opportunity otherwise known as the Silver Economy. Our analysis showed that this consumer target was growing in number and had a higher level of disposable income than other demographic segments.

And so, I gathered a group of cross-functional people from across the organization who were going to help move this forward. Typically, we would have dived straight into idea generation. However, this time, I decided to shake things up, and start by getting each person to visit and talk to some older adults in their homes.

Whilst all of these visits were rich in terms of learnings, mine turned out to be truly eye-opening. I headed to an apartment in the north of Paris to meet with a lady, Marie, who was a fan of our product category, bottled water, and was also a loyal consumer of one of our brands. Marie was delighted to talk to me at length about her life, as well as her food and beverage habits and preferences.

After a while, her voice grew raspy and I politely suggested that she take a sip from the bottle that she had been holding in her hand during our discussion. She agreed that this was a good idea, before proceeding to open the bottle... with her teeth!

Visibly shocked by what I had just seen, Marie quickly justified this by explaining that she suffered from arthritis in her arms, which meant that she no longer had the strength to open bottles with her hands, and therefore used her teeth, which were now the strongest part of her body. The caps on the bottles were simply too tight for her to open them in any other way.

As my face clearly still looked slightly shocked, she then went on to reassure me that it wasn't just her who opened bottles in this way, but also all of her friends too. Our discussion continued, and Marie proceeded to highlight several other problems which she experienced with our products and the wider beverage category.

At that moment I realized the critical importance of making the time and effort to get out of the office and meet with real customers in their real-life environment to better understand their real-life experiences. The reality of what I saw and heard by visiting Marie that day, namely several significant pain points with our products, was in stark contrast to the rosy view of consumer experience I previously had whilst sitting in the ivory tower of our beautiful head office on one of Paris's most iconic boulevards.

It is the undertaking of these simple real-life connection moments that should be at the heart of customer-centricity for a business, rather than any customer values statement hung on the office wall.

This experience also taught me that formal customer research, whilst a critical part of an innovator's arsenal of tools and techniques, is not sufficient. After all, we would probably not have identified Marie's issue within a focus group discussion in a research facility, or through a questionnaire or survey. We would not have thought to probe a problem that we didn't know existed, or that the customer may not have spontaneously mentioned, thinking that there was no other solution available.

This experience was at the genesis of the Immerse and Inquire step.

—

Objective

The objective of this Immerse and Inquire step is to capture clues about our core customers' real-life needs, wants and pain points today. These clues will provide the solid foundation we need for building a successful innovative offer.

Why is this step so important?

There are two key reasons why this step is so important:

- ✓ An innovation can only be successful if we succeed in changing customer behaviour. And it is very difficult to change customer behaviour without deeply knowing and understanding the reality of their lives and experiences today.
- ✓ For a customer to change their behaviour, our innovative offer will need to respond to a real-life need or want. And the simplest way to truly understand customers' needs and wants is to engage with them directly.

What are the key risks if you skip this step or do it badly?

There are two key risks:

- You may base your innovation project not on facts, but on assumptions which are old or incorrect.
  In many large organizations there are beliefs around customer needs which have been regurgitated so many times that they have taken on the status of truths which now remain largely unchallenged.
  However, not only do customers and their needs change over time, but the learnings about their

needs often become distorted over time (remember that game called Telephone?) Or the learnings are extrapolated incorrectly to customers or countries not included in the original research, for example.

- Given that customer understanding is the foundation for any innovation project, building a project on a weak or fragile foundation almost inevitably leads to a weak or fragile result, meaning that there may not ultimately be a customer need for your new offer.

Surely this is an infrequent and exceptional situation, which would only happen to stupid people, right? Wrong. It happens every day.

In the entrepreneurial world, there being no customer or market need for the product or service is consistently in the top reasons why startups fail. There is no evidence to show that startups are founded or led by stupid people – on the contrary, in fact. They are simply humans who have fallen too easily in love with their specific offer idea, forgetting that their startup will only succeed if a customer is willing to pay for it, because it will fulfil a need for them.

In the corporate world, this situation often manifests itself in what is commonly known as 'techno-push', where a technical team has invented a new technical solution, which then gets passed to the Marketing and Sales teams to 'just sell'. Don't get me wrong, new technologies can be a brilliant enabler of innovation, but I wish you good luck if you expect the technology to succeed in-market without really knowing why your customer should care, or what's truly in it for them.

Steps to success

In this step, you will gather customer clues to help you answer the following two power questions:

> **What are the biggest outcomes
> our core customers want?**
>
> **What are the biggest obstacles
> our core customers face
> when trying to achieve these outcomes?**

Clearly your focus for these and subsequent power questions is the frame that you fixed in the previous step.

Let's start by defining the two types of customer clue you will be looking for, **outcomes** and **obstacles**.

Outcomes

Outcomes refer to the end result that your customer actually wants, rather than the means that they may use to get that outcome today. This notion, originally called *Jobs-to-be-Done*, was pioneered by Harvard Business School Professor Theodore Levitt when he famously said: 'People don't want to buy a quarter-inch drill. They want a quarter-inch hole!'

Taking this logic one step further, the desired customer outcome was not actually a hole, but rather having a picture attached to the wall. This is the outcome that they *really* want.

On the surface, this may appear to be semantics. But no – it brings huge benefits to innovators.

Focusing on outcomes helps you to sharply identify customers' *real* needs, maximizing the probability that you will address them through your new innovative offer.

Taking the drill/hole analogy a step further. Imagine that a new startup launches which allows a customer to get a quicker, cheaper or easier hole in the wall – or even allows them to attach a picture to the wall more quickly and easily with no hole. Customers are likely to flock to adopt this new solution, rather than continuing to purchase drills. The drill company who is blindly focused on perfecting their drill is likely to suffer.

Remember that the same phenomenon has already happened in the photography industry: the desired customer outcome of capturing memories can now be quickly, easily and cheaply achieved using a smartphone, with little need for a separate camera.

When trying to identify outcomes, asking 'Why?' a few times can be a simple and effective way of drilling down to identify the customer's true desired outcome.

For example, 'I want a new skin cream', may drill down to 'I want to look better', which may drill down to 'I want to feel more confident when talking with potential dates', which may drill down to the real outcome of 'I am desperate to find love'.

This deeper articulation of the customer's desired outcome will provide a much more powerful springboard on which to build an innovation project.

Obstacles

Obstacles are things which actively prevent or hinder your core customer from achieving their desired outcome. This could mean things that slow them down, make it more complex or costly, or create negative emotions such as frustration. In other words, these are things which cause some kind of physical or emotional pain, albeit the level of pain can be small and does not have to be severe.

Obstacles can include difficulties, tensions, irritants, inconveniences, points of friction and sources of dissatisfaction. In short, anything that is suboptimal for them, which could also include things such as expensive pricing.

Given that innovators are often positive and optimistic by nature, and the culture of many large organizations is often collaborative and consensual, there can be a natural aversion to talk openly about obstacles that your customers face, given their inherent negativity.

However, you must absolutely go out and find customer obstacles and also talk about them internally! Obstacles are very powerful to an innovator, like gold dust. After all, if you can identify real-life obstacles, and find ways to help your core customers to overcome them in a way which is profitable for your company, then you are very likely to succeed with your innovation project.

To reinforce this point, let's think about a successful business like Uber. Of course, some of Uber's success is directly linked to its technical solution, namely its digital app. However, I would argue that most of its success has been generated through a deep understanding of the obstacles faced by customers when using the existing solutions, in this case traditional taxis.

Hard to find a taxi? Obstacle overcome: with Uber, the car comes to you. Worried that the taxi driver is going to rip you off by taking the long route? Obstacle overcome: with Uber, the final price and route are announced and paid for upfront. Need a specific size or type of vehicle for your journey? Obstacle overcome: with Uber, you get to choose between several different vehicle categories, including more sustainable options.

For completeness, I should mention there are actually a few exceptions to this, when you will focus uniquely on outcomes, and not obstacles. For example, when working in the luxury market. Luxury handbags help to project a positive image of the customer and their status – the outcome – but don't really need to overcome any obstacles to create value for the customer.

For the rest of this step, we are going to focus on identifying outcomes and their associated obstacles. It is the combination of both outcome and obstacles which will provide the solid foundation for our innovation project.

Moving onto the three sub-steps to help you gather outcome and obstacle customer clues:

LISTEN

OBSERVE

QUESTION

LISTEN

The term *listen* here is not used in the sense of listening to audio content, but rather in the sense of actively making an effort to listen to what's going on around you. The key power question to guide you here is:

> **What customer clues already exist that we can capitalize on?**

Whilst it may not always feel like it, the truth is that there is an abundance of customer clues which already exist in your ecosystem on which you can capitalize for your innovation project. This might mean looking for existing customer research (and, yes, I know that commissioning new research is always sexier, right?) This might mean making the effort to better connect with salespeople within your organization to identify what customers' needs and preoccupations are, or what questions customers are asking right now.

This might mean doing some online search or online listening, going where your customers are online – whether on your own or by asking a specialist agency to do this on your behalf. Whilst clearly not everything that exists online is true or helpful, for most industries there is a treasure trove of customer clues just waiting to be discovered. This has become even easier and more efficient thanks to the ever-increasing performance of AI-powered tools.

Last but not least, there are often industry-wide resources available which provide customer clues, including specialist industry press, industry reports, industry associations, industry events and conferences, or indeed specific industry experts. Whilst these resources are also available to your competitors, and can sometimes appear somewhat superficial, they can still be helpful for two main reasons.

They can help you to double-check that the clues that you will gather directly from customers are representative of your wider core customer target. And their analysis can also be useful for identifying future trends that will affect your customers, helping to ensure that your innovative offer will bring value and remain relevant for many years to come.

OBSERVE

The second sub-step is observing: making an effort to see and better understand what's going on in real-life today. The key power question to guide you with this is:

What are our core customers currently doing?

This technique may seem simple; however, it is incredibly powerful for innovators when collecting customer clues. Let's look at why. If I ask you to tell me exactly what you ate for dinner four days ago, and precisely how you cooked it, would you be able to?

The reality is that humans (which include your core customers!) often aren't able to accurately recall or articulate what they do, because much human behaviour is unconscious and habitual. So there can often be inconsistency in what they say and what they actually do. It can therefore be much more effective to observe customers 'live' and in real time to capture clues, rather than to ask them questions after the event.

To get the most accurate and useful clues, try to observe customers undertaking their *usual* way of achieving an outcome, at the place and time where they *usually* do this.

For example, if you work for a breakfast cereal company and are interested in how people energize themselves in the morning before going to work, the best option would clearly be to observe your core customers at home before they go to work. What do they do? What do they eat? What do they drink? Who are they with? How much time do they spend? What do they struggle with? And so on. This is likely to give you much deeper and richer learnings than if you asked this person to tell you about their morning routine during the evening within an artificial focus group setting.

Try to observe customers as if through a child's eyes, which means with a high level of curiosity, and zero judgement. Try to capture each of the key steps of the journey your customer takes today to achieve the outcome, in chronological order. It is really important that you capture their journey from the very beginning (for example, when the customer realizes that they have a need, or when they make the decision to buy a product or service), right through to the very end (for example, this could be using or consuming the product or service, recycling the packaging, or reviewing their experience online).

QUESTION

Once you have completed your observation and understand what your core customers *do*, it is time to go more deeply beneath the surface, to try to understand *why*. The key power question to guide you here is:

> **Why are our core customers doing what they are doing?**

Questioning customers helps us to find great clues and allows us to get to the deeper understanding that we need to build a high-performing innovative offer. Here are two recommendations to help you lead this stage in the most effective way:

First, do your questioning *after* your observing, where possible. This keeps the observations pure and unbiased, and also enables questioning based on what you have concretely observed.

I learned this lesson the hard way: when I worked for a leading food manufacturer towards the beginning of my career, I undertook an Immerse and Inquire session with a mum at her home in London. I did the questioning first, and she proudly told me how healthy her family's eating habits were, how much fresh fruit and salad they ate, and how her children never snacked on treats – all of which turned out to be completely untrue as soon as I looked inside her kitchen cupboards, which were full to the brim with cakes and chocolate!

Second, start with customer context. Whilst it is very tempting, try not to jump directly into questions about the key area of interest from your frame. Follow how professional researchers conduct interviews, by starting with broader questions about the customer and their lives in general.

Not only will this help to warm up your customer and build trust but, more importantly, it will give you valuable context about their responses and minimize any risk of misinterpretation. In the food example above, the learnings that I would have taken away from looking in the customer's cupboard would have been quite different if she had been diabetic, was married to a body builder, if she had nine children, or was a vegan. Context contextualizes customer clues.

Top tips

✓ Undertake the OBSERVE and QUESTION sub-steps as a pair. This allows one of you to lead the customer interaction, whilst the other one writes down everything you learn.
Make sure to write *everything* down. You will see and hear so much rich information that, if you don't make detailed notes, it will be impossible for you to retain and use your learnings in an accurate way.

✓ During the OBSERVE sub-step, look around at the context of your customer: the room they're in, what's around them, the other products and services that they buy – these are valuable additional clues.

✓ During the QUESTION sub-step, try not to talk too much, and don't be afraid of silence. Pauses will encourage your customer to talk more. Also, focus on asking open questions; i.e. questions which require more than a yes or no answer. This will encourage customers to open up and give you fuller and more detailed answers.

✓ When you identify obstacles, try to capture them as precisely as possible. What *exactly* is the problem? Why is it a problem? Where and when do they have the problem? What impact does the problem have?

✓ When you're writing down what customers say, capture it verbatim; i.e. exactly what they say, with no editing, adaptation or interpretation. At this step, your single-minded focus is on capturing the raw material.

✓ If possible, and with the customer's permission of course, record your OBSERVE and QUESTION sub-steps using your phone, which allows you to refer back to this material afterwards.

✓ Even if this step feels uncomfortable for you, or makes you nervous, don't forget to smile! Remember that your customers are just human beings. Relax and enjoy the interactions.

Lessons from leaders

One company that has always inspired me as best-in-class regarding Immerse and Inquire is P&G, one of the largest consumer goods companies in the world, behind leading blockbuster brands such as Pantene, Olay, Tide, Ariel, Fairy, Febreze, Always and Tampax.

Right from the beginning of my career as a junior marketer, I was fascinated by stories from my peers about customer-centricity at P&G not being a mere principle, but rather an attitude which was lived and breathed.

This attitude has led to P&G being a pioneer of immersive ethnographic *in situ* research, where they go into consumers' homes to directly observe them living their daily lives – whether in the kitchen, laundry room or indeed bathroom. This approach has led to many success stories over many years.

In one such study in the 1970s, consumers were observed opening detergent packets with screwdrivers and razors. This was not necessarily seen as a problem by consumers as that was the way that it had always been. However, the observation of this customer obstacle led P&G to invent their patented consumer-friendly 'easy-open box'.

In another example, an *in situ* researcher observed that liquid laundry detergent would pour down the side of the front of the bottle when poured, which led to the invention of a 'dripless spout' – and millions of dollars in increased sales.

In fact, this same customer-centric attitude was at the genesis of the hugely successful Pampers brand. While watching his first grandchild, a P&G researcher realized the mess of cloth diapers and the need to carry them around until returning home. This real-world observation led to him and fellow researchers developing a better and more affordable disposable diaper, which has been a staple for consumers ever since.

A.G. Lafley, former CEO of P&G, and strategic adviser Roger Martin, who doubled P&G's sales, quadrupled its profits, and increased its market value by more than $100 billion in just 10 years, summarize this neatly as follows: 'you must truly get to know your consumers – to engage with them beyond the quantitative survey, through deeper, more personal forms of research – watching them shop, listening to their stories, visiting them at home…' (Lafley and Martin, 2013).

Actions to accelerate

Here are the top three actions to help you move forward quickly:

1. Block time in your diary for the LISTEN sub-step, and make sure that this is also scheduled in the diaries of every taskforce team member.
2. Recruit some core customers – either through a professional customer recruiter, or through your network (but, in this case, make sure they are not too close to you or your company to be biased).
3. Undertake your OBSERVE and QUESTION sub-steps in the real-life environment of those core customers, at a time of day that's most relevant to your innovation project.

6

Step 3: Narrow the Need

N

Ever since I was a kid, I've been fascinated by the topic of health, and this has been a recurrent theme in much of my work over the past 25 years. This has involved missions as diverse as working for Boots, one of the world's leading health retailers, organizing events with healthier brands from iconic companies such as The Coca-Cola Company, developing communication campaigns with WW (formerly known as WeightWatchers), partnering with Disney to inspire kids to develop healthier habits, and also launching exciting new healthy beverages. I've always loved the idea of businesses helping people to lead healthier and happier lives. And it was this business world of health which helped me to grasp the true power of insights.

Rewind back to 2004, and the Kellogg's brand Special K launched a high-profile communications campaign, with the enticing promise that women could drop a jeans size in just two weeks. As a 28-year-old guy, I was clearly not in the core customer profile, and therefore not interested from a personal perspective. However, from a business perspective, I was intrigued about why this campaign was so successful. The answer comes back to outcomes and obstacles.

In terms of outcome, Special K had done a great job. The promised outcome of losing weight was highly desirable for their core customers, and was expressed in a fresh, visual and emotionally engaging way. In terms of obstacles, Special K had clearly understood that losing weight is often tough, often takes a long time and also requires significant effort. And so the attractive promise of being able to lose weight by simply replacing two daily meals with Special K cereal for just two weeks was always likely to succeed: in short, customers get the outcome they want but without the obstacles. They were enabling their customers to get what they want via a path of least resistance.

The success of this Special K campaign came from them leveraging the intersection of outcome and obstacles: in the marketing and innovation world, this is called an insight. For this campaign, a simplified version of the insight might have been something like:

Women really want to lose weight [outcome], but this is often tough, taking a long time and requiring significant effort [obstacles]

Fast forward over 20 years, pharmaceutical phenomena such as Ozempic and Mounjaro have achieved great commercial success from leveraging a very similar insight, making weight loss even easier.

An insight crafted in such a way, expressing both a customer outcome and its associated obstacle(s), provides a strong springboard for creating innovative new offers, whatever the industry. Take Amazon, for example. Amazon helps you get almost any product you can think of [outcome], without needing to wait a long time, without the effort of having to go to the store, or the worry about if you're paying a fair price [obstacles].

If you identify the outcome your core customers want, what obstacle(s) they are facing today to achieve that outcome, and then create a solution which helps them to achieve it in as friction-free a way as possible (and in a way which is profitable for you), you are highly likely to succeed. Success follows strong insights.

This is the Narrow the Need step, so let's get cracking!

—

Objective

The objective of this Narrow the Need step is to prioritize customer needs on which to build your innovative offer, from the many customer clues gathered in the previous Immerse and Inquire step. You will craft an **innovation insight** which captures the biggest outcome your customers want and the biggest obstacle(s) they face to achieve it.

Why is this step so important?

There are two key reasons why this step is so important:

✓ This step helps you to prioritize the most important customer clues amongst the large number which you gathered. This prioritization is important to enable you to focus your innovation time and efforts on those customer needs which are the biggest and most significant, and will therefore create the greatest value when fulfilled.

✓ This step starts the journey of transforming the customer clues you have gathered into your innovative offer. Without this step, the time and energy spent to understand your core customer in the previous step will not create any tangible business value. After Immerse and Inquire, you must systematically ask 'so what?'

What are the key risks if you skip this step or do it badly?

There are three key risks:

• Without effective prioritization of customer needs, there is a greater risk that you will waste time, energy and money working on projects with lower business potential.

The customer's willingness to pay for your innovative solution will ultimately be in proportion to the degree to which you help them; i.e. how much you make their life better. Meaning that your reward will be greater if you tackle a big and significant customer need.

- Your innovative project is likely to lack sharpness of focus. Whilst this would not be an issue if you had unlimited innovation time and resources, this is rarely the case, meaning that your time and resources will simply be spread more thinly. Less focus, less time and fewer resources often means that a project is more likely to flounder and die.

- The innovative offer you create may not end up solving a real-life problem for real-life customers at all. As previously mentioned, this happens frequently, and is a common reason for failure of many innovation projects, in both corporates and the startup world.

  As humans, we have a tendency to fall in love with our own ideas, which can distract us from what our customers may actually need. Your priority should always be to fall in love with your customers' outcome and obstacle(s), rather than your desired solution, as this will help keep your project moving in a great direction.

Steps to success

In this step, you will answer the following power questions:

> **What is the biggest outcome
> our core customers want or need?**
>
> **And what are the biggest obstacle(s) they face
> when trying to achieve this?**

Clearly your focus for this step is still the frame that you fixed in Step 1.

The three sub-steps to help you with this are as follows:

COLLATE

CONNECT

CRAFT

COLLATE

The very first thing to do is to collate all of the customer clues that you gathered during Immerse and Inquire in the same place so that you can have easy visibility over all of them with your taskforce team.

There are several ways to do this depending on the way in which you have captured your customer clues. It may be pulling your handwritten or printed paper notes all into one place or putting them all together on one virtual whiteboard. The important point here is that you can easily and clearly see all the different clues you have gathered within one field of vision.

Whilst somewhat macabre in name, one of the most powerful techniques here, especially if your taskforce team is all together in one physical place, is what I call a 'murder wall'.

Think back to all of the police detective series you have seen on TV. The detectives all use one technique to help them solve the crime: sticking all the clues they have gathered (names, photos of suspects, locations, motives, etc.) onto a large wall in the police station, so that they can see all of the clues together easily at a glance.

CONNECT

The second sub-step is to make connections between the customer clues in front of you, in order to identify those outcomes and obstacles that are the most significant and most recurrent amongst the customer clues that you gathered. The power questions here are:

> **What are the biggest outcomes**
> **that our core customers want?**
>
> **And what are the biggest obstacles**
> **that they face to achieve them?**

This prioritization of outcomes and obstacles is important, as it will have a direct impact on the level of value that you will bring to your core customer, and therefore also your company. In simple terms, if you help a customer to achieve an outcome which is significant for them, by removing obstacle(s) which are significant, you are more likely to create significant value for your company.

If your customer clues are physical pieces of paper or sticky notes stuck on a murder wall, then you can easily bring similarly themed clues together, or make connections by drawing lines between them with a marker. If you're working on a virtual whiteboard, you can simply drag and drop to connect similar clues together to cluster them, or connect them using lines or arrows.

If your clues have been captured in electronic format, AI can help with this. Simply feed your electronic document(s) into an appropriate AI tool, and prompt it to provide a summary of the most common and significant outcomes (for example, 'Based on this material, what are the biggest outcomes, end-results or jobs-to-be-done that our customers want?') and obstacles (for example, 'Based on those biggest outcomes, end-results or jobs-to-be-done, what are the biggest obstacles and pain points that our customers face?').

CRAFT

Once you have created these connections and prioritized, it is time to craft your innovation insight. The good news is that you have already done most of the work for this.

Start by selecting the most significant or common outcome you identified in CONNECT. Next, find the most significant and common obstacle(s) that your core customers experience *to achieve that specific outcome.* To craft your innovation insight, you simply need to connect this outcome and obstacle into a simple, sharp sentence which follows this structure:

**Based on what we saw and heard
during Immerse and Inquire,**
[our core customers] **really want/need**
[biggest outcome]
**BUT the key obstacle(s) they face
to achieve this today is** [biggest obstacle(s)]

By expressing your innovation insight in this way, you are effectively highlighting the key 'gap' or 'tension' for your customer (which they may be consciously aware of, or not). It is this gap or tension which your innovative offer will ultimately fill or resolve, thus creating value for both your customer and your company.

Make sure that there is indeed a gap or tension in your innovation insight – you can check this by making sure that there is a 'but'. If there isn't, which is a common mistake, it is much more probable that your innovative offer won't solve a problem for your core customer, therefore making it much more difficult for your company to generate value.

—

Let's look at an example. Imagine that you're working for an ice-cream company who would like to innovate. As part of your Immerse and Inquire, you connected with a group of core customers you call Conscious Champions: female and male, aged between 30 and 40, who are passionate about health, fitness and also the environment. (I've simplified the description of the core customer here, for clarity.)

The biggest outcome you identified was that they were looking for a quick, refreshing and sweet way to end their meals. Their biggest obstacles were that the majority of pre-prepared desserts are often high in sugar, high in fat, and use a lot of single-use disposable plastic packaging.

So you might craft your innovation insight as follows:

**Based on what we saw and heard
during Immerse and Inquire,
Conscious Champions really want a quick,
refreshing and sweet way to end their meals**

BUT the key obstacles they face today are that most pre-prepared desserts are high in sugar, high in fat, and use a lot of single-use disposable plastic packaging.

As a team, draft multiple innovation insights, as it's really tough to write a perfect one first time. Then review them together to see which one(s) are the strongest. To check if you have got a strong insight, ask the following two power questions:

Does this insight reflect something important for our core customers that they truly care about?

Does this insight reflect something which is relevant, attractive and actionable for our company to address through innovation?

Make sure to also double-check that the innovation insight that you prioritize is relevant to the frame you fixed in Step 1.

Once you have crafted one innovation insight that you are happy with, you are ready to move on to the next step.

Top tips

✓ If you captured your customer clues on paper, use highlighter pens to increase the visibility of the most important points. It can make this step much more efficient.

✓ Instead of relying on the internal opinion of your taskforce team regarding which of your innovation insights is the strongest, share them with some of your core customers, and see which one resonates most.

  If it's a strong insight, they will typically say something like 'that's me', or 'that's exactly how I feel', or 'you've understood me so well'. If there's no reaction at all, this is a sign that your insight is not strong enough and needs to be reworked.

✓ Be careful not to confuse outcome and offer. The outcome is the end result that your core customers want; the offer is the means, the product, service or solution that will help them achieve this. Only include the outcome in the insight, *not* ideas for what the offer might be.

✓ If you're struggling to get to a strong innovation insight, it is possible that you didn't collect enough or strong enough customer clues in Step 2, Immerse and Inquire – in which case it might be useful to go back and work on that step more fully.

Learnings from leaders

Starbucks fully understood the importance of innovation insights when they launched their pioneering Mobile Order & Pay service in 2015.

  Their customers loved their daily Starbucks experience, but the long in-store queues were a major obstacle or, as their Chief Digital Officer described it, 'pinch point', when on the go and in a hurry to get their favourite drink.

Their solution, which still exists today: wherever they are, customers can use the Starbucks app to find their closest store, customize their favourite beverage and pay for it. And when they arrive at store to pick up their order, they don't have to wait in line, they can simply grab their coffee and go, making their coffee run much faster and more convenient.

This digital innovation proved highly successful, sped up service and boosted customer satisfaction. Starbucks knew exactly what their core customers wanted, and the obstacle they faced, and then created a way to help them get it in as friction-free a way as possible – and a way which also generated significant business for them.

Interestingly, their offer was guided by an observation that 15% of Starbucks purchases in the US were being made with phones – which was remarkable at that time when paying by phone was still the rare exception. This meant that Starbucks had built up a highly valuable collection of linked credit cards, which enabled a seamless shift from pay-in-store to pay-in-app.

Of course, Starbucks has further evolved their services since then to also include delivery, enabling you to get the coffee you love without going to the store at all.

In their own words: 'By pairing coffee and convenience, now there's always time for that Starbucks run.'

Actions to accelerate

Here are the top three actions to help you move forward quickly:

1. Block time in your taskforce team's diaries to review all of the customer clues gathered during the Immerse and Inquire step. Make sure to book a room which is sufficiently large, light and away from distractions.
2. COLLATE all customer clues from all members of the taskforce team in advance to allow you to focus your time and energy during the session on the CONNECT and CRAFT sub-steps.
3. Plan some time in your diary after the session to get feedback on the innovation insight(s) you crafted – ideally from your core customers but, as a bare minimum, from colleagues who are close to your core customers.

7

Step 4: Nail a Northstar

N

At the beginning of my tenure as Global Innovation Director, I was working with colleagues on an innovation project of which the frame was to encourage children to drink more water rather than the plethora of highly attractive, less healthy soft drinks. The brief given to the Research & Development team had been blunt and broad: something along the lines of 'How might we make a better water bottle for kids'.

This brief led to a multitude of small incremental ideas – from different coloured caps, to peelable stickers, and special inks on labels. It was not that these ideas were bad (in fact, we ended up successfully deploying many of them on temporary brand activations); it was just that they weren't significant enough to truly change children's drinking behaviour.

It was then that I understood the direct correlation between the quality of the brief and the quality of the ideas that are generated. The reason that we often struggle to succeed with innovation projects is that the brief is not good enough to generate ideas that are good enough.

For example, have you ever been to a creative brainstorming session which was highly enjoyable, with a high level of enthusiasm and energy, but where very little happened with the ideas afterwards? Highly likely that this was not an issue with poor facilitation techniques, or the laziness of the project team post-workshop, but rather that the brief had not been articulated with enough rigour or precision.

However, just having a clear brief is not enough: we also need to make sure it is highly ambitious. Highly ambitious briefs lead to highly ambitious ideas.

Going back to our project of healthy hydration for kids. After months of struggle on the project, we changed our articulation of the brief. If we really wanted to change kids' behaviour, we needed to make our offer as desirable as possible to them. What do kids find the most desirable? Toys. So what if, instead of the banal 'How might we make a better water bottle for kids', we decided to work on the much more ambitious 'How might we make drinking water as enjoyable as playing with a toy?'

That seemingly simple word shift and strong increase in ambition unlocked the project in an instant, putting it on the trajectory to success. Instead of being bound by the codes and constraints of the world of bottled water, we now found ourselves immersed in the world of kids – especially toys, games, characters and movies – being inspired by what they *truly* found most desirable.

Having then followed similar steps to those outlined in the remainder of this book with the cross-functional taskforce team, we developed an innovative product code-named 'Mascot': a range of children's favourite movie characters who had magically been transformed into water bottles!

Understanding what kids *really* love led to my signing a global partnership with Disney, our Spanish team launching a best-in-class pilot which, once proven to be successful, became an award-winning multi-country project, generating millions of dollars of revenue. But, most importantly of all, the success of this project led to kids drinking more healthily, thereby fulfilling the mission that we had fixed in the frame at the very beginning.

This successful experience from writing better and more ambitious briefs was at the genesis of the Nail a Northstar step.

—

Objective

The objective of this Nail a Northstar step is to define and align on a specific brief, and to make it as bold and ambitious as possible. You will use this to generate a large quantity of truly innovative and customer-exciting offer ideas in the next step.

Why is this step so important?

There are four key reasons why this step is so important:

✓ It will enable you to generate bigger, bolder and more ambitious ideas, which go beyond any old or existing ideas that you may already have in mind.

✓ It maximizes the proportion of the ideas you will create which are truly relevant to your customer and business needs. It will ensure that your idea generation is effective, efficient and focused, thanks to the sharpness of your innovation insight crafted in the previous step.

✓ It helps ensure that your innovation project is moving in a direction which is fully aligned with company strategy, goals and priorities; i.e. your frame.

✓ This step also helps you to be sure that offer ideas generated will be sufficiently new and differentiated vs. the company's offer today, and also any projects which may already be in the pipeline.

What are the key risks if you skip this step or do it badly?

There are two key risks:

• You are likely to waste significant time and energy in the next step, Open up Options. Because, unless your innovation brief is sharply boxed, you will generate ideas in more of a scattergun approach, meaning that a large proportion of them will simply miss the target, be irrelevant, and therefore ultimately be discarded.

I continue to be amazed how frequently this happens: after all the brainstorming sessions and sticky notes, sometimes most of the brainstorm output is thrown directly in the bin, simply because the brief was not sufficiently well defined. This not only causes frustration for project leaders who feel like they have got many fewer options than they thought they had, but also for participants who have given their time and energy.

- In the next step, you are likely to generate smaller and softer ideas, which lack power and potential. As mentioned above, idea generation from a brief which is bigger, better and bolder will necessarily lead to innovation ideas which are bigger, better and bolder. However, the opposite is also true: a smaller and softer brief will lead to smaller and softer ideas, and therefore reduced project performance and impact.

Remember that any company is ultimately looking to maximize return on investment (ROI) from its offers and its people, and the same is true of the time, energy and resources that we dedicate to innovating. A smaller and softer project with lower potential may require similar time and resources to develop as a project of much higher ambition and potential. I call this notion return on innovation investment (ROII).

Steps to success

So, in this step, you will transform your innovation insight into a clear and ambitious brief. I call a clear and ambitious brief a **northstar**, hence the title of this step. Just like the northstar, we are looking for a brief which is specific, clear, attractive, inspiring and helps guide you towards a bold and ambitious destination.

Your northstar will consist of just one element: a power question beginning with the words:

How Might We…?

It is a northstar, with its 'How Might We…?' question, that you will use to generate innovative offer ideas in the next step, Open up Options.

The 'How Might We…?' formulation for your northstar is very important, especially the word 'might'. 'Might' keeps people's minds much more open to creative, unexpected and breakthrough solutions, compared with words like 'can' (which makes us think about feasibility), 'would' (which makes us speculate on specific conditions), or 'should' (which makes us think that we are under obligation).

Moving onto the three sub-steps to help you create a powerful northstar:

ASPIRE

BENCHMARK

CHOOSE

ASPIRE

In this first sub-step, your task is to write as many 'How Might We...?' questions as possible based on your innovation insight. Especially if you've never done this before, it's unlikely that you'll be able to write a perfect 'How Might We...?' question first time, so it's best to write several alternatives without being overly concerned about their quality at this stage.

Building on the innovation insight from our Conscious Champions example in Chapter 6, possible options for your northstar might be:

How Might We...

**... create the most delicious and healthiest dessert
for Conscious Champions?**
**... enable Conscious Champions to enjoy
a zero-plastic dessert?**
**... help Conscious Champions to refresh their palate
in a sweet yet healthy way?**
**... help Conscious Champions to enjoy
a guilt-free sweet treat at the end of meals?**

As you can see, sometimes the northstar may not capture all angles of the innovation insight, and that is fine at this stage.

To make a northstar as ambitious and aspirational as possible, try to use superlative words, for example,

**How Might We create
the best/fastest/most etc.?**

Superlative words bring the highest possible level of ambition, helping you to create the most aspirational northstar, and therefore generate the most aspirational and impactful ideas in the next step.

As we saw in the kids healthy hydration example above, do not include your existing offer in your 'How Might We...?', as this is likely to generate ideas which are only incrementally better than the solutions which exist today. One way of checking this is to ensure that you have not used comparative words, such as bett<u>er</u>, fast<u>er</u>, <u>more</u> or <u>less</u>. For example, don't write:

How Might We...

... create a range of healthier yogurts?
... create a range of desserts with less packaging waste?

By injecting your current product or service into your northstar, you are effectively weighing your brief down, anchoring it to today's reality, and therefore depriving yourself of the opportunity to reach bold, creative and disruptive solutions.

Building on this, it is important not to write any offer as part of your northstar. For example, don't write:

How Might We...

... create a range of fat-free yogurts for Conscious Champions?
... create healthy creamy desserts in paper-based packaging?

If you do this, the narrowness of the question will lead to a narrowness in the offer ideas generated in the next step, thus depriving you of being able to generate the large number of diverse ideas that you will need to succeed.

Conversely, you do not want your northstar to be too broad, or the offer ideas that you create will also be too broad vs. your frame. This leads to a high risk of ideas not being relevant and therefore being discarded. For example, don't write:

How Might We…

> **… create healthy, sustainable meals for Conscious Champions?**
> **… revolutionize packaging for desserts?**

It is also important to ensure that the focus in your northstar always remains on your core customer, rather than 'the market' or your company's internal objectives. So don't write:

How Might We…

> **… capture more market share in the pre-packaged desserts category?**
>
> **… capture a greater share of the fridge in retail stores?**

BENCHMARK

Once you have written several 'How Might We…?' questions, it is time to move onto this next sub-step, where you are going to identify some best-in-class benchmarks to make your northstar bolder, brighter and even more ambitious.

Your objective here is to write some additional 'How Might We…?' questions based on your innovation insight. However, this time, each question will make reference to a benchmark company, brand or solution which is specifically best-in-class at the key elements you captured in your innovation insight. To help with this, you can use the following power question:

How Might We… as well as [benchmark]?

Let me share a real-life example to illustrate this. I was once supporting the innovation efforts of a cosmetics company which had retail stores. One of their innovation insights was that their core customers enjoyed being able to browse and try all of the different cosmetics products in-store, but got really frustrated that the staff who worked there looked bored and didn't make them feel welcome.

Thinking about well-known best-in-class benchmarks which could make our northstar as bold, bright and ambitious as possible, we asked ourselves Who is *truly* best-in-class at welcoming people? Various options were discussed, but the clear consensus of the taskforce team was that Disneyland was globally recognized as *the* best-in-class at welcoming customers.

So the northstar we wrote, which turned out to be incredibly effective, was:

How Might We…

… make our stores as welcoming as Disneyland?

Going back to our Conscious Champions example, we could write northstars such as:

How Might We…

… create a healthy dessert which tastes even better than Oreo cookies?
… create a dessert which is as environmentally friendly as an apple picked from a garden?

The benchmark is exactly that: a benchmark. It does *not* mean that the ideas that you would create in the next step need to involve Oreo cookies or apples. In these examples, it is the tastiness and the environmentally friendly aspect of these benchmark examples which help make those northstars highly ambitious.

And do not worry if the northstars you write seem unrealistic (After all, can there be anything more delicious than an Oreo cookie?!) As per the quote often attributed to Norman Vincent Peale, the American author best known for popularizing the concept of positive thinking, 'Shoot for the moon. Even if you miss, you'll land among the stars'.

Write as many northstars with best-in-class benchmarks as you can.

CHOOSE

Now that you have written several northstars, it is time to choose the strongest ones. To help you choose, you can use the following power questions:

Which northstar is most closely linked to
our innovation insight?

Which northstar is the clearest and sharpest?

Which northstar will enable us to generate
the maximum number of ideas?

Which northstar is the most ambitious,
motivating and exciting?

You also need to double-check that the northstar you choose will generate ideas for offers that are truly relevant. To do this, ask yourselves the following power questions, thinking about the offer ideas you are likely to generate based on the northstar:

**Will they be relevant offers
for our company?**

**Will they fit well with the company strategy,
goals and priorities?**

**Will they be sufficiently new, differentiated and
innovative vs. the company's offers today,
and initiatives which may already be
in the pipeline?**

**Will they be big enough opportunities
for our company to prioritize
and invest sufficient time, money
and resources into?**

At the end of this step, you need to have at least one strong northstar. It is possible that you may have a few more that you also feel are very strong, which potentially touch on other angles of your innovation insight. You can undertake the next sub-step, DIVERGE, on as many strong and relevant northstars as you have prioritized – this will help you to generate the maximum number of ideas.

Top tips

✓ Write northstars as a collaborative taskforce team session – ideally in person, but online can also work, if necessary.
Start the session by writing northstars individually and in complete silence, which helps to capitalize on the collective intelligence and different perspectives of each member of the taskforce team. Afterwards, share them in pairs and small groups to compare and contrast, before collectively prioritizing the strongest one(s).

✓ If you use a benchmark in your northstar, make sure that everyone in the taskforce team both knows the benchmark and agrees that it is relevant to use as a best-in-class benchmark.

✓ Make sure that the northstar(s) that you prioritize is attractive, and inspires you personally and as a taskforce team. This will certainly help you deliver to the best of your ability in the next step.

Learnings from leaders

When many people think of McDonald's, innovation isn't always the first word to come to mind. However, the story of the origins of McDonald's is a best-in-class example of Nail a Northstar in action.

The McDonald brothers, Richard and Maurice, reportedly had a specific and bold goal: they aspired to be able to serve their customers' food orders in 30 seconds, rather than the traditional wait time of 30 minutes in other restaurants at that time.

It was this highly ambitious goal which led to them developing the 'Speedee Service System' in 1948: an innovative approach which significantly streamlined and accelerated kitchen operations and food preparation, inspired by the benchmark of assembly line efficiency.

In 1954, their focus on efficiency and speed caught the eye of Ray Kroc, a milkshake machine salesman, who saw the huge potential of this system and subsequently transformed this small burger restaurant in California into the global leader that we know today.

At the time of writing, McDonald's has more than 36,000 restaurants in more than 100 countries. A great example of the power of setting a specific and highly ambitious northstar to create a disruptive and relevant new offer.

Actions to accelerate

Here are the top three actions to help you move forward quickly:

1. Block time in your taskforce team's diaries to transform your innovation insight into northstars, all starting with the words 'How Might We...?'
2. Pre-prepare some simple templates with 'How Might We...?' written on them, to make it easier for your taskforce team to capture several different northstars.
3. Make sure to leave enough time at the end of the session to choose which northstar is the strongest. Ask taskforce team members to individually evaluate the different options using the power questions above, before sharing your thoughts all together and aligning.

8

Step 5: Open up Options

When I founded Innovinco® in 2017, our core mission was based on a northstar: 'How Might We help the world's leading corporations to maximize business growth by accelerating innovation?'

I had personally experienced how difficult it can be to innovate successfully within large organizations – even within organizations that were serious in actively wanting to innovate! – and so wanted to help those people who were in similar positions as I had been, capitalizing on key success factors I had learned along the way.

Whilst I didn't realize it at the time, my natural reflex was to follow the norms of the industry; i.e. I would create Innovinco® in the standard mould of an agency or a consultancy.

However, there was one significant thing that gnawed at me about this: namely that these kinds of operating models were often designed more for the benefit of the company, rather than for the benefit of their customers.

I'd certainly experienced this in my time working on the corporate side; for example, sales pitches from the world's leading consultancies, led by senior partners who seemed to magically disappear as soon as the business had been won. The client work was systematically passed to a team of inexperienced consultants, who often had zero real-life experience of working inside a large corporation, let alone any real-life experience of leading a successful innovation initiative.

This reflection led to a pivotal moment for my company: the realization that I needed to open up my thinking to the huge number of potential options and opportunities that were available.

For the following five years, we generated and explored a huge variety of different business options and opportunities, all fully aligned with our north-star: from bite-sized consultancy modules, e-learning, e-coaching, in-person and virtual training programmes, one-to-one coaching, large-scale innovation events with over 200 people... nothing was really off-limits if it could help people in large organizations to move innovation forward at pace, and also generate significant value for Innovinco®.

To the outside world, it may have appeared that we were adopting a slightly erratic scattergun approach – otherwise known as throwing spaghetti at the wall to see what sticks. Whereas, in reality, we were opening ourselves up to a wider range of options and opportunities than most of our competitors and systematically testing them (in ways that you will see in the next chapter). We knew that the higher the number of options we explored, the higher the probability of finding a very high value opportunity for our customers and our company.

This approach was accelerated thanks to Innovinco® being based at Station F, the world's largest startup campus, for over two and a half years. Having been selected to be part of one of the leading incubation programmes, we had the privilege of being surrounded by 3,000 other startuppers every day.

Given my corporate background, it suddenly felt like opening up to an Aladdin's cave of opportunities such as subscription models, freemium, franchising and licensing, as well as everything related to the sharing economy.

I found the breadth of potential options and opportunities that could be generated by our northstar brief thrilling. It quickly became clear that there was a direct correlation between the quantity of idea options that we generated and the quality of our ideas. And, as we will see later, this proved to be a winning approach for Innovinco®.

This experience was at the genesis of the Open up Options step.

—

Objective

The primary objective of this Open up Options step is to generate a very high number of diverse ideas which respond to your northstar. Once this is done, you will prioritize those ideas, before defining and articulating your highest priority idea in a much sharper and more specific way.

Why is this step so important?

There are three key reasons why this step is so important:

✓ This step enables you to generate a large number of ideas which are fresh, disruptive and truly innovative. It stretches your thinking and maximizes the diversity of options you will consider, thus presenting you with a greater number of potential options from which to choose.
More potential options mean a higher-quality thinking and evaluation process about which one will be most highly performing.

✓ When executed well, this step enables you to fully capitalize on the collective intelligence of the team. There is much research, including that from award-winning journalist and best-selling author Matthew Syed, on the power of a diverse team to deliver higher-quality outputs. This makes logical sense, as clearly no one individual has the monopoly on good ideas, and each team member brings their unique perspectives.

✓ This is the step in which you are actually going to identify the offer which delivers against your core customers' needs. So, the better you do it, the higher the probability of project success.

What are the key risks if you skip this step or do it badly?

There are four key risks:

- You are very likely to jump too quickly onto existing, old or obvious ideas, which may not be the strongest ones. If you fall into this trap, you are likely to miss ideas which are potentially stronger at creating value for both your customers and your company.
- Especially when working in large organizations, you or your team may default to only generating safe ideas. Without realizing it, you may tend to subconsciously apply filters which kill any ideas that might be controversial, difficult to implement, too costly, that might be tricky to operationalize, or might be rejected by your boss. This reduces your ideas to the lowest common denominator, diluting the size, scale and business potential of your project.
- You may inadvertently use emotion and subjectivity to prioritize and choose the best ideas, rather than a more objective and rigorous approach. In a world now dominated by social media, we have got into the habit of 'liking' things without too much thought or consideration. It can create

problems if we adopt a similarly loose approach when it comes to choosing innovation ideas.

- Lastly, unless you specify your innovation idea sharply enough, there may be significant ambiguity around what your idea actually is. After all, a few words on a sticky note is not enough to clarify all key aspects of an offer. Unless specified, there can be issues with internal alignment and offer development later on.

Steps to success

So, in this step, you will use your northstar to open up your thinking and generate many different options for potential offers. From those options, you will then prioritize and define the strongest offer idea(s), based on which will bring most value to your customers and your company. In this step, you will be working towards answering the following power question:

> **What innovative offer idea do we think is strongest for core customers and our company?**

As always, there are three sub-steps to help you to achieve this:

DIVERGE

CONVERGE

SPECIFY

DIVERGE

Your first task is to generate the maximum quantity of ideas that you can, without any evaluating, prioritizing, judging, filtering or clustering. The large quantity is very important to maximize the probability of generating powerful and winning ideas and also ones which are fresh and less obvious. Think about it: if you have just one idea, then the statistical probability of that one idea being great is very low. However, if you have one million ideas, then the statistical probability of having one great idea is very high. Successful idea generation is simply a numbers game!

In my experience, one of the most effective methods to succeed here is brainstorming. Brainstorming is often used as a generic term for idea generation; however, it actually refers to a specific methodology which can be highly effective if deployed in the right way.

The three key ingredients for an effective brainstorming session are:

1. A facilitator: to prepare, lead and animate the session, and keep it on track.
2. A small group of participants: in my experience, three to six participants is the sweet spot. Even better, multiple small groups of participants who can work in parallel. The small size of the group ensures that each participant actively contributes, and multiple groups working in parallel enables you to multiply the number of ideas generated – which, as mentioned above, increases

the statistical probability of you identifying great ideas.

3. Your northstar from the previous step, which focuses your brainstorming efforts by forcing you to create ideas which respond to a specific 'How Might We...?' question.

Building on point 2 above, some additional guidance about participants:

- Try to maximize the diversity of the participant profiles within each small group, as this will maximize the diversity of the ideas generated. And I mean diversity in all senses: gender, age, background, function, job type, level of experience and so on.

- Be careful with inviting senior members of the organization if there is a risk that their ideas will dominate, or if the other participants are likely to be less creative due to their presence.

- Depending on the nature of your industry or innovation project, it can be very helpful to invite core customers to participate in this type of idea generation session, so that they can co-create offer ideas with you. This approach brings the benefit of injecting greater customer-centricity, which should lead to stronger and more relevant ideas.

  If you decide to adopt this customer co-creation route, try to invite what are sometimes known as 'super customers'. These are customers that not only fit your core customer profile, but who are also able to articulate their thoughts and ideas with high levels of creativity and clarity. They are not 'better' customers but rather customers that can contribute more to this kind of session.

And make sure that all of the relevant documentation is in place *prior* to the session, with support from your legal team. This may be as simple as a Non-Disclosure Agreement (so that the customer is less likely to discuss what they have seen and heard after the session) and/or an intellectual property release form (which means that they can have no personal claim to the intellectual property of any of the ideas created during the session).

My recommendation is to ensure that this paperwork is proactively shared with the customers in advance of the session to give them enough time to read and digest it and not feel pressured to simply sign it just before the session starts. Of course, to thank them for their time and contribution, and for their signing of these documents, it would be highly appropriate to offer a small gift or monetary incentive.

Now that our three key ingredients are in place, let's review the three key elements of the brainstorming process:

1. Write your chosen northstar 'How Might We...?' question in large easy-to-read bold letters on a flipchart or whiteboard.

    One of the key mistakes that people often make when brainstorming is not to explicitly write the brief of the brainstorm somewhere everyone can see it. This inevitably leads to a greater number of off-track, less relevant ideas which will ultimately be rejected.

2. Hand out a block of sticky notes and a marker pen to each participant.

   Having led these sessions hundreds of times, I've found that Post-It branded 'Super Sticky' sticky notes, square-shaped and in the standard pale yellow colour are most practical and effective. And, in my experience, Sharpie branded fine point markers are the best for writing ideas due to the readability of the ink vs. a ballpoint pen or standard felt-tip.

   For more recommendations of the specific materials I use for brainstorming sessions and other innovation workshops, head over to **InnovatorKit.com**

   Encourage the participants to write legibly by writing in capital letters, rather than joined up cursive lower-case writing, which can be notoriously hard to decipher. Ideas which can't be easily read rarely get read and are therefore very likely to end up in the idea graveyard.

3. The brainstorm is officially started by the facilitator, and the participants start to generate as many ideas as possible. Each idea is written on one sticky note. As soon as a sticky note is written, the team member reads it out to share it with the team, before sticking it onto the flipchart or whiteboard. The reading out of each idea helps to spark further new ideas within the group. And the brainstorm carries on until you feel you have no more ideas to respond to your northstar.

   Very important: there must be no discussion, evaluation, judgement (whether positive or negative), prioritizing, clustering or filtering at this stage as this will stop the creative process and limit the number of ideas you generate. Your only objective is quantity of ideas at this stage.

Formally ban any comments or discussion about whether an idea is good or not, whether it's feasible, whether it would be approved by management etc., otherwise participants' brains will switch into evaluation and analysis mode, rather than the open and creative mode we need here. The mantra of 'no idea is a bad idea' is true here – as long as the idea responds directly to the northstar, of course.

Encourage the participants to generate specific and tangible ideas. You are looking for ideas of specific offers that the company could potentially put in place, for example new products, services and solutions. Many participants will have a natural tendency to write down broader themes such as 'convenience' or 'sustainability' which, whilst potentially relevant, are not specific or concrete enough to be actioned. They are simply too broad and generic.

Before moving to a group brainstorming format, I recommend to start with a short individual brainstorming in silence. This can be a really powerful technique for three main reasons:

✓ It ensures that everyone actively contributes to the idea generation from the start, including those quieter or more introverted participants.
✓ It helps you to generate a very large number of ideas very quickly. For instance, let's say that each participant can individually generate 10 ideas

within three minutes. If they're working in a group of five people, that means 50 ideas generated in just three minutes.

✓ This is a great way of enabling participants to empty their brain of all the existing ideas they may have, and so give them more time and opportunity afterwards to focus on creating brand new, more disruptive ideas.

I recommend to close an initial round of brainstorming on a northstar after approximately eight minutes. Any longer than this, and I've found that the participants get tired and the energy drops very quickly, as well as the quantity of ideas being generated.

However, after just eight minutes, clearly you will not have the high quantity of ideas that you need. So, when the energy drops and the idea flow slows down, it is the perfect moment to introduce a new technique: brainstorming with constraints.

Brainstorming with constraints is a very powerful way of injecting new energy into a brainstorm session, as well as generating a higher quantity of fresher and even more disruptive ideas. This method is simple, yet brilliantly effective.

Participants still generate ideas which respond directly to their northstar 'How Might We...?' question. Except that now, each idea generated must *also* respect a specific constraint. My favourite constraints to use for this include (with full credit to the d.school team at Stanford who taught these to me):

**Each idea must cost over
1 million pounds/dollars/euros to implement**

(or 1 billion pounds/dollars/euros if you work in
a company or industry with lots of money!)
**Each idea must contain some element of
fantasy or magic**
(i.e. what would Harry Potter do)
Each idea must get you fired by your boss!

You can no doubt see how these constraints can
unleash a heightened sense of freedom and creativity,
and open the participants up to explore some more
fresh and disruptive options.

Use each constraint to brainstorm for three to five
minutes before moving on to the next one. Only use
one constraint at a time; i.e. they are not cumulative.
Whilst some of the ideas generated through using these
constraints may be unrealistic, this technique helpfully
stretches participants' thinking, which leads to more
disruptive ideas which could indeed be realistic.

To help you to generate even more ideas, here are
a few additional 'What if...?' power questions which
can also work well to uncover potential new ideas for
your northstar (again, to use one at a time):

**What if we put ourselves in the shoes
of our biggest competitor?**

**What if we put ourselves in the shoes
of a startup?**

What if we exploit cutting edge technology?

**What if we innovate in 'how'
we deliver our offer?**

> What if we borrow and build on ideas
> from other industries?
>
> What if we borrow and build on ideas
> from other countries?
>
> What if we better capitalize on innovations
> from our partners and suppliers?
>
> What if this was our own company?

CONVERGE

Once you have generated a large quantity of ideas (I typically recommend at least 100), it is time to review, organize and prioritize them, to identify which one(s) is most valuable to take forward to the next stage. This action of narrowing down the options is called 'convergence'.

It is really important to truly separate these DIVERGE and CONVERGE sub-steps. More specifically, it is important not to start to CONVERGE whilst you are trying to DIVERGE, as the human brain is not capable of effectively managing these two very different activities at the same time – even if you're an expert multi-tasker.

To organize your ideas, I recommend that you start by clustering together those ideas which are identical or very similar, and give each cluster a short, sharp, descriptive name which you can write as a title with a marker in capital letters (or the electronic equivalent if you are working on a virtual whiteboard).

Next, it's time to evaluate and prioritize each idea and any clusters of ideas. The quickest and most effective way I have found to do this, especially within a workshop setting or taskforce team meeting, is the Attractive/Accessible matrix, below:

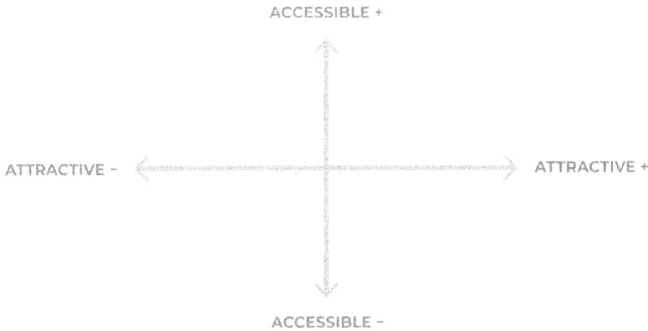

ACCESSIBLE +

ATTRACTIVE −   ATTRACTIVE +

ACCESSIBLE −

Each idea and cluster of ideas is individually evaluated on two criteria: Attractive and Accessible.

Attractive

To evaluate whether an idea is Attractive, ask the following three power questions:

How attractive do we believe this idea will be to our core customers?

To what degree do we believe this idea will help them achieve their key outcome and remove their key obstacle(s)?

To what degree do we believe that our core customer would be willing to pay for this idea?

In an ideal world, you would make this evaluation with the involvement of real core customers. Do this if you can, as it brings more robustness and rigour to the prioritization of your ideas. However, if that is not possible, given that you are going to Verify the Value of your prioritized idea(s) in the next step, it is OK for your prioritization here to be based on your existing customer knowledge, hypotheses and assumptions.

Accessible

To evaluate whether an idea is Accessible, ask the following three power questions:

> **How accessible or feasible would this idea be for our company to implement?**
>
> **To what degree does this idea leverage our company's existing assets, knowledge, capability or infrastructure?**
>
> **To what degree do we estimate that this idea would require an acceptable level of investment for our company and deliver a sufficient level of profit?**

One comment regarding feasibility: it is important to be as objective as possible here, as many ideas are much more feasible to implement than you might initially think – especially if you consider potentially working with partners.

Always evaluate Attractive before Accessible, as it is the more critical criterion – after all, it doesn't really matter if an idea is Accessible if it's not Attractive to your core customers!

After discussion and alignment with all brainstorm participants or taskforce team members, each idea and cluster of ideas is placed in the corresponding position on the Attractive/Accessible matrix above.

Unsurprisingly, it is those ideas which are placed in the top right-hand quadrant (i.e. perceived as both highly Attractive and Accessible) which should be prioritized in the first instance, as these are the ones which should enable you to deliver greatest value to customers and your company in the easiest way.

However, also keep a note of those ideas which are Attractive but currently less Accessible (i.e. bottom right-hand quadrant) as these are potential longer-term innovation ideas for your pipeline.

SPECIFY

Once you have prioritized your lead idea (which was most likely located in the top right-hand corner of the Attractive/Accessible matrix), it is time to transform this idea into a more sharply articulated offer. Scrappily written ideas on sticky notes are often not very clear and can be unhelpfully ambiguous regarding what your idea actually is; hence the importance of articulating it as a more specific offer.

To do this, you can use the following power questions with your team. Some of these require you to think back to your frame, and also previous steps focused on your core customers, to ensure that there is full alignment:

Customer profile:
**Who specifically is the core customer
for our offer?
Is the buyer the same as the beneficiary?**

Customer need:
**What is the key customer outcome
behind our offer idea?
What is their key obstacle(s)
to achieving this outcome today?
What evidence do we have that this is
a large and significant customer need?**

Customer offer:
**In one short and simple sentence,
what is our offer?
How does our offer work concretely?
How does our offer leverage our company's
strengths, assets, capability
and competitive advantage?**

Customer growth:
**How will our offer create strong growth
for our company?
Against which one of the four growth goals
will our offer mostly deliver?**

| BUY MORE | MORE OFTEN | PAY MORE | MORE CUSTOMERS |

Offer differentiation:
**How is our offer different and better
than what already exists today?
Is this differentiation linked to
primary customer needs?**
i.e. is the way in which our offer is different
bringing our core customers significant value
with regards to their outcome or obstacles(s)?
**What are the three specific major advantages
that our offer brings?**

Offer business model:
**In one short and simple sentence,
how does our offer actually make money?
Is there just one revenue stream, or multiple?
Are there secondary financial benefits?**
For example, would there be a positive business
benefit on other offers in our range?
**What are the big costs or investment
that would be involved?
Are we confident that our new offer
would not cannibalize our existing business?**

Offer implementation:
**How would we 'deliver' this offer?
Where would we sell this offer?
Where would core customers buy this offer?
Would we work with key partners or suppliers?
What key resources would we need?**

By asking, discussing and answering these power
questions, your specific offer will soon take shape – an

offer which creates value for both your customers and your company, both of which are critical success factors for your innovation project. It is normal that you won't have a perfect or final vision at this stage – these elements will be tested and refined as you move forward through the next steps.

As you detail your offer, you may discover that your initial idea is too big and broad and would be better split into two or three separate offers. In which case, complete this SPECIFY sub-step for the strongest offer(s) that you want to move forward to the next stage.

It is also possible that this sub-step may uncover that your idea is perhaps not so strong. Again, no big problem. If the offer idea you originally prioritized cannot be salvaged, go back to your Attractive/Accessible matrix and choose the next strongest idea, and go back through this SPECIFY sub-step.

To finalize this sub-step, I recommend to write a short and simple summary, focusing on the key customer-oriented elements, structured as follows:

To help [your core customer]
to achieve [their desired outcome]
more easily by removing [obstacle(s)]
we recommend to test [sexy name of your offer]
which is a [type of product, service or solution]
which [what your product or service does]

The three specific reasons why our core customer will want to buy, use or consume this solution more than existing solutions are
[the three key competitive benefits]

—

It might be tempting to think that the innovation process stops here now that you've got an idea. However, you're only halfway through the process! You must continue through to the end to make sure that your project delivers value for your company and your customers in real-life.

Top tips

✓ Try to organize brainstorming sessions outside of the participants' standard working environment. This helps to create a separation from their day-to-day reality which can often stifle creativity and disruptive thinking.

✓ Where possible, encourage the participants to stand during brainstorming as this brings much more dynamism and energy than people sitting back and slouching in their chairs.

✓ If you hear people evaluating ideas during a brainstorming session, you can use the yellow and red card approach from football to get them to change their behaviour, in a clear yet light-hearted way. Show them the yellow card for their first and second 'offences'. On the third offence, show them the red card, which means that they need to sit out of the session for five minutes.

Learnings from leaders

It seems inconceivable today that Lego, one of the world's largest toy manufacturers, was in severe financial difficulties in the early 2000s. A key part of its subsequent successful turnaround can be attributed to an Open up Options approach, where they generated and prioritized a huge quantity of ideas.

One of their key initiatives here was Lego Ideas, launched in 2008: an open innovation community where Lego fans can submit their own ideas for new Lego products, and vote for other members' ideas. Members collect votes for their ideas online, and ideas that receive 10,000 votes have a chance of being selected to become part of Lego's product portfolio.

In the first 10 years, the Lego Ideas platform grew to become a global community of over 1 million members, who submitted over 26,000 ideas for new Lego products. Of these, 166 ideas received over 10,000 supporters, and 23 official Lego Idea sets were launched. It is unsurprising that such a customer-centric approach which celebrates the passion, creativity and talent of their fans has been so successful.

However, Lego does not only rely on getting ideas from the outside – it also has a large pool of internal talent, supported by best-in-class infrastructure.

In 2024, Lego broke ground on a 50,000 sqm Innovation Campus at the LEGO Group global headquarters in Billund, Denmark. This new building will house 1,700 creative colleagues from across product marketing and development, gaming, product and quality teams, including the company's 600+ designers, in one space to create future Lego experiences that will inspire children and adults across the globe.

Actions to accelerate

Here are the top three actions to help you move forward quickly:

1. Block time in your taskforce team's diaries, as well as other relevant people who can contribute to a brainstorm session, to transform your northstar(s) into offer ideas. Wherever possible, book a room outside the office, to help the participants to think more creatively.

2. Pre-purchase a large number of sticky notes and marker pens. Prepare a large sheet with your northstar 'How Might We...?' written in large letters to stick on the wall, to maximize the probability that the ideas generated will be relevant, and also another large sheet with the Attractive/Accessible matrix. Alternatively, these can be written on a whiteboard or flipchart, if these will be present in the room. And don't forget to buy some drinks and snacks to keep energy levels high!

3. Make sure to take photos of your ideas at two key stages of the session – after the DIVERGE sub-step when all ideas have been generated, and after CONVERGE when ideas have been prioritized. This means that you will have a visual record of this work, even if the sticky notes fall off the wall or, even worse, are thrown away by the cleaner.

9

Step 6: Verify the Value

V

Back in 2016, I had the privilege of being trained by the Stanford University d.school in Design Thinking, the problem-solving and innovation methodology which inspired several elements of the INNOVATOR Way®. The d.school team had decided to take their iconic bootcamp training programme outside of the Stanford campus for the first time, and so I found myself heading to the vibrant city of Hong Kong.

Far from being theoretical, this training programme was based on a real-life business challenge: for this edition, our task was to develop a new offer for Millennials for the leading airline Cathay Pacific. One of their senior leaders briefed us before we undertook a series of team exercises to understand consumer needs, generate ideas and build offers.

One exercise stood out. Having generated ideas, and prioritized one of them, we were given around 30 minutes to create a low-resolution prototype of our offer. Furthermore, if that wasn't enough pressure, we were then effectively thrown out of the building where the training was taking place, to go and test our offer directly with our Millennial core customers on the streets of Hong Kong. Not such an easy task, especially when we didn't know the city or anyone in the city, and didn't speak Cantonese!

Armed with a flipchart pad, each page of which was a hand-drawn representation of a screen of the mobile app we had imagined, we quickly found two young women eating pizza on a café terrace, who were more than happy to give us feedback on our offer idea. Twenty minutes later, we had gathered a significant quantity of evidence from core customers about our offer idea – what was working well and less well – all gleaned with a minimal amount of preparation time, and zero budget.

It was at that moment that I realized the phenomenal power of low-resolution prototyping as a means of both sharpening an idea, and as a means of testing its real-world value to potential customers. Having always worked on market-leading iconic brands where everything always had to be perfect, this rough and ready technique seemed quite alien and uncomfortable to me. However, on that day in Hong Kong, and proven many times since then during client programmes, this experimental approach has paid dividends.

Furthermore, this experience taught me just how important proactive and frequent check-ins are with core customers throughout the life of any innovation project. Not just one round of testing.

Especially within larger organizations, we can tend to want to keep everything about our project under wraps to enable a big bang launch, and also protect confidentiality. However, this approach carries significant risk, as any incorrect assumption along the way can easily derail the whole project. It is heartbreaking to see how many times this still happens, with these offers dying quickly after launch, and therefore effectively wasting all the time and energy (as well as blood, sweat and tears!) that have gone into them.

As I learned in Hong Kong, it is highly effective to adopt an iterative 'prototype, test and improve' approach. By running pragmatic experiments with core customers, you can quickly gather real-life evidence of whether or not your offer creates value. This approach not only enables much faster progress on projects, but also de-risks them.

This experience in Hong Kong was at the genesis of the Verify the Value step.

—

Objective

The objective of this Verify the Value step is to gather real-life evidence regarding whether your innovative offer is desirable to your core customer and also check viability from a financial perspective. The evidence gathered will provide robust guidance regarding whether to move the project forward, to improve it, to pivot or indeed to kill it.

Why is this step so important?

There are three key reasons why this step is so important:

✓ It enables us to de-risk a project. The more real-life evidence you gather before launch, the lower the risk of project failure after launch. This is especially important in a context where many innovative projects carry a high level of risk, and also involve a high level of investment, time and resources.

✓ This step helps to ensure that we remain customer-centric, which, as we saw earlier, is a critical factor in innovation success. Checking the desirability of your offer with your core customers necessarily means remaining close to them.

✓ Conducting multiple rapid experiments using simple prototypes allows the project to move forward in an agile and efficient way, helping you to move forward fast and without losing momentum.

What are the key risks if you skip this step or do it badly?

There are three key risks:

• You create significant risk of wasting time, money, energy and resources on developing and launching offers that ultimately won't work. Whilst this happened a lot in the past – hence the frequently cited statistics about the high proportion of innovative new products and services which fail – I believe that this is no longer acceptable today. If an offer's going to fail, you must ensure it fails as early as possible.

There have never been more tools at an innovator's disposal to test offers quickly and cheaply – both in person and online. The customer desirability of *any* innovative product or service can easily be checked, quickly and cheaply, amongst a large sample of core customers, thereby strongly de-risking the project.

- Even if your offer does not fail when it launches onto the market, not adopting a test and learn approach can lead to a solution which is not fully optimal, as a result of not capturing opportunities for improvement during offer development.

  This step helps you to understand which features are really important for your core customers and must absolutely be part of the offer, vs. those nice-to-have features which are less important, or potentially not valuable at all. It will also help you to identify any missing features which are important for your core customers, and also features that you might want to integrate at a later date.

  Not implementing this step, or not implementing it well, therefore carries an opportunity cost in terms of the quality of the innovative offer you launch.

- Not adopting this kind of approach means that your project may simply move forward too slowly.

In the past, this may not have been so important. However, in today's world moving at the supersonic speed of startups, speed of execution can often be a critical success factor.

Speed is also important in terms of managing a team; in my experience, it is often harder to keep team energy, enthusiasm and focus on any project beyond 18 months. No one wants to be part of a team where the project just seems to be dragging on, without any clear end in sight.

Steps to success

In this step, you will test your offer to check whether it will bring a sufficient level of value to both your target customer and your company. To do this, we will adopt the mindset and behaviours advocated by methodologies such as Design Thinking, agile, lean and sprint. The power question to focus on in this step is:

> **Will our offer idea bring enough value to core customers and our company?**

As always, there are three sub-steps to help you do this, and this time they are iterative:

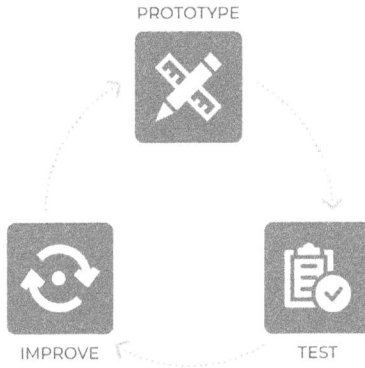

PROTOTYPE

IMPROVE   TEST

PROTOTYPE

Now that you have specified your innovative offer idea, it is time to create a low-resolution prototype of it. The word 'prototype' may seem quite technical, but the idea here is very simple. The power question you can use is:

How can we make a quick, simple and cheap prototype to bring our offer idea to life?

The objective here is to create something which helps you to quickly and clearly communicate your offer idea to your core customers. This will enable you to get their feedback and check that your offer idea is desirable and would create value for them if launched.

There are two key reasons why creating a low-resolution prototype is so powerful.

First, creating a two-dimensional or three-dimensional representation of your offer idea makes it much sharper than words on a page; to create the prototype, you will need to discuss, define and align on many elements about your offer idea with your taskforce team. This is especially important as different people can interpret words differently: 'large' for one person might mean the size of a chair, whereas for another it might mean the size of a building!

Second, because your offer idea is clearer and more sharply defined, the feedback which your core customers will be able to give you about your offer idea will also be clearer and more sharply defined, and therefore higher quality and more valuable to you.

The key to succeeding with this is to create your prototype as quickly and cheaply as possible. Whilst this may sound hard to believe, I've not yet encountered an innovative offer idea that can't be prototyped in less than one hour, at zero cost! This speedy and low-cost approach is very important, as it will allow you to test and iterate your offer idea more times and therefore get more feedback than if you have to invest significant time and budget to create higher-fidelity prototypes.

What different types of prototypes can you create? Well, prototype formats can be visual, physical or digital. They can be illustrations, storyboards, prototypes made with craft materials, sales brochures mocked up with PowerPoint or Canva, videos created on your mobile phone… the list is almost endless.

Whilst you may consider this type of home-made prototype to potentially look a bit rough, the whole point here is that your prototype should *not* be perfect, but rather just good enough to communicate your offer idea.

Online platforms powered by AI also now enable you to create prototype visuals and videos very quickly, easily and cheaply, with no designer or specialist skills required.

TEST

Now that you have created a prototype of your offer idea, it is time to test it with your core customers. Depending on your company, industry and offer idea, you may need to do tests with the beneficiary, the buyer, or both.

There are two main objectives: first, to test the desirability of your offer idea to ensure that it will indeed bring value to your core customer. And, second, to ensure that the value created for your customer will translate into a willingness to pay which is sufficient to achieve the business objectives which you wrote in your frame – after all, that is the reason why you started this project in the first place. In short, through these tests, we are looking for proof of value, for both customer and company.

The way to test remains very much in the same spirit as when you were prototyping: you are going to run fast and cheap experiments with your core customers, using your prototype, of course. The objective is to get some real-life quantitative data and also valuable qualitative feedback, as a means of identifying your core customers' level of appreciation of your offer idea, as well as its perceived strengths and weaknesses.

What kinds of test can you do? Well, the basic principle is simple: you need to show your prototype to a number of your core customers, whether in person or online, and ensure that there is a simple mechanism to capture their feedback, both quantitative and qualitative. There are many ways to do this: from face-to-face interviews, to online surveys, or mocked-up landing pages. As previously mentioned, your primary focus here is tests which are fast and cheap.

The temptation here can often be to simply ask core customers whether or not they like your offer idea represented by your prototype. Whilst this is better than not speaking to customers at all, this approach can provide input which can be inaccurate, as what people declare and what they would do in real life is often very different.

In my experience, if you go up to someone and ask them if they like or would like to buy something, more often than not (and often after a moment's hesitation) that person declares, 'yes'. But the reality is that, despite their positive answer, they would *not* actually choose or purchase it in real life: they probably said 'yes' to be polite, or to avoid any potential awkwardness or embarrassment. So the data from tests where your core customers only declare their intention should be treated with caution.

Better tests start with an open, neutral question which will encourage your core customers to provide a more spontaneous and rich response, not force them into making any binary yes/no decision, nor introduce any kind of bias into their response. Here are some power questions that you can use:

What do you think about this?

**Are there any elements that are valuable
for you? Why?**

**Are there any elements that are less valuable
for you? Why?**

How could we make this more valuable for you?

Would you buy this? If so, why? If not, why not?

The best tests require a small 'sacrifice' on behalf of your core customer, some so-called 'skin in the game' when it comes to your offer. It is this small sacrifice which gives confidence that your core customers' intentions are indeed to purchase or use your offer.

What are small sacrifices? In my experience, there are four types which work really well: asking for money, asking for time, asking for contact information, or asking for commitment.

Asking for money is exactly that, asking for some level of monetary deposit. If your core customer is prepared to pay this (as you are probably not yet at the stage where you can actually accept a monetary payment), then you can safely assume that they would indeed be interested in purchasing your offer.

You can also ask them how much they would be willing to pay for your offer. Asking this question can give you a clearer idea of the level of value that they perceive your new offer will bring to them. Simply put, if customers aren't prepared to pay what you need to make this project successful for your company, you won't create sufficient value for your company to achieve your frame; i.e. it is not viable.

Given that many people perceive themselves as time-poor, if your core customer is prepared to give you some time – for example, for a follow-up information call, a meeting or a webinar – this is also a strong indicator that they have a genuine interest in purchasing your offer.

Given how protective we all are now about our personal data to avoid unwanted and spam communication, if your core customer is prepared to give you their contact information (for example, address, email address, mobile number), this can also be considered a positive test result.

To ask for commitment, you can ask your customers for a simple written confirmation that they are interested in purchasing your offer. This could include securing a pre-order or succeeding in getting them to sign a letter of intent. This does not have to be binding or fully commit them to purchase (which would be a significant hurdle for them to jump over based on just a prototype) but acts as a simple written proof that confirms that they are serious.

This type of test can provide very useful quantitative data: for example, the percentage of core customers you speak to who are prepared to make a small sacrifice. To ensure that you make decisions in a robust way, set the success threshold for this percentage *before* you run the test, otherwise it can be difficult to decide what to do based on the results.

This type of test is also incredibly helpful for providing you with a lot of very useful qualitative feedback, which can be used during the next sub-step, IMPROVE.

Test with as many core customers as possible, to ensure that the inputs and feedback that you get are as representative as possible. However, input from just a few core customers is still better than speaking to no customers at all. When you are finding these customers, ensure that you don't introduce bias by speaking to people who already have a link to you or your company – as these people are obviously likely to be more positive about your offer idea.

If you struggle to find core customers to test with, social media can be very helpful (as long as you are careful not to introduce any bias by testing with people you know, as mentioned just above). Simple posts such as 'I am looking for dog owners, living in London, who are open for an informal 20-minute discussion over the next two weeks' can be surprisingly effective. Often, they won't expect or require any recompense, over and above a nice coffee and a slice of cake.

When you are testing, it is important to truly listen to what your core customers say, rather than pushing or selling your offer to them. Hard as it is, you must temporarily forget that you are in love with your offer idea. Don't desperately try to convince them that it's great or selectively listen to just those elements of feedback that you want to hear.

Approach testing conversations with a truly open mind, rather than a desire to get your offer idea positively validated at all costs. If your core customer gives constructive or negative feedback, definitely don't become defensive, otherwise they are unlikely to give you any more feedback, for fear of upsetting you further.

See all feedback from your core customers as their way of helping you – whether that's helping you to make your offer idea even better, or indeed flagging that your offer idea might be risky. You asked for their opinion, so you must listen to their response. In any case, see their feedback as feedback on the project, rather than any personal judgement of you.

Negative feedback is a warning signal and should be listened to appropriately. Yes, it might not be serious. However, it might represent something very serious that you ignore at your peril. The best way to know for sure is to test with more core customers to get a more representative view.

If there are specific aspects of your offer which are critical to its success *and* you don't know how core customers will react to them, this makes them higher risk. Make sure to proactively probe these during the TEST sub-step. Initially, see if core customers mention these risky aspects spontaneously. If they don't, it's probably a good sign, but be sure to specifically probe these aspects, to see how core customers react and what feedback they provide.

I recommend to undertake testing in pairs so that one of you can lead the testing discussions with the customer, and the other can listen and observe, as well as capture notes and learnings.

If possible, and with their permission of course, try to record what your core customers say and do during testing, using your mobile phone. This material can be very helpful for you to refer back to afterwards and can also provide very powerful evidence to show to stakeholders about your offer idea. After all, it is much more credible for them to see what your core customers say about your offer, than just to listen to your (invariably positive) thoughts and opinions.

This recorded material is also very useful to help you start to talk about your offer in the same way and in the same language that your core customers use. This will be highly valuable at the ACTIVATE sub-step for creating communications that talk about your offer in a relatable and relevant way.

As this kind of 'do-it-yourself' testing approach is less common in large companies, here are a few pointers which may be helpful:

If, as with many innovation projects, the stakes are high (for example, if there will ultimately be a large amount of investment required to bring your offer to market), it will be important to *also* run some formal customer research at this stage, led by an expert professional customer research agency.

I recommend to discuss this with your customer research experts as early as possible, so that they can already shortlist some strong research agencies. These agencies will typically test your offer idea with a larger sample size of your core customers, using deeper quantitative or qualitative methodologies, to provide a formal and final customer verdict.

Just to be clear, the need to do formal research in no way removes the high value of the PROTOTYPE, TEST, IMPROVE approach. They are complementary. The PROTOTYPE, TEST, IMPROVE approach is great for developing and iterating your offer. Formal research is often necessary to provide confidence to key stakeholders that it is an offer idea worth supporting and investing in.

During this TEST sub-step, make sure that your manager is aware and OK for you to show your offer idea, including prototypes, to core customers outside your company. Do not take this risk on your shoulders. Common sense applies in terms of managing confidentiality and competitive risk; do not leave behind any elements of your prototypes with core customers, especially if these could be easily shared on social media, for example.

Whilst this is not always necessary, and depending on the number of core customers you will speak to, you may want to use a simple non-disclosure agreement to discourage them from discussing what they have seen. However, this obviously adds a layer of time and administrative complexity, and these documents, even when signed, are often not completely legally watertight. Your legal team can help determine the best approach.

IMPROVE

The final sub-step here is that of improving your offer idea in line with the learnings gained from your core customers. The key power question is:

> Based on our tests with core customers, what can we improve so our offer helps them to achieve their desired outcome more easily?

Depending on the TEST feedback from your core customers, you may be required to make smaller or larger improvements to your offer idea.

Depending on the scale of the changes required, you may be able to modify your existing prototype, or you may need to create a new one. Either approach is fine, so long as the prototype being tested is easy for your core customer to understand and give feedback on.

There is, of course, the possibility that core customers see so little value in your offer idea that it doesn't make sense to IMPROVE. In which case, go back to the previous step, Open up Options, and select an alternative strong offer idea to PROTOTYPE and TEST. Make sure to use the learnings from your previous tests to help guide you on which offer idea is most likely to bring your customer the most value, and bring most value to your company.

—

As mentioned above, these three sub-steps – PROTOTYPE, TEST and IMPROVE – are iterative; i.e. you need to repeat this loop of action until such time as your quantitative TEST results are positive, and you have addressed any negative feedback or potential risks that were mentioned qualitatively.

Before moving onto the next step, Achieve the Ambition, ensure you are confident that your core customers are both willing and able to pay for your offer at a level that will meet the business objectives defined in your frame.

Top tips

✓ Always have some craft materials for low-resolution prototyping around your office or workplace. This means that you are much more likely to adopt this prototyping approach on a regular basis than if you need to go out to the store specially. If you want to see the prototyping materials I have in the office, head over to **InnovatorKit.com**

✓ When you are capturing feedback from your core customers, try to capture what they say verbatim; i.e. the exact words that they use, with no interpretation. This is the most useful raw material to collect for making decisions about your project later.

✓ If customers ask questions about your prototype, for example, 'Where do I press?', don't answer them but rather ask the question back to them, 'Where would *you* press?', which will give you valuable feedback about your solution and how to improve it.

✓ If you decide to test your prototype online, there are a number of service providers and digital platforms which can help you do this. Head over to **InnovatorPicks.com** to see my latest recommendations.

Learnings from leaders

The Verify the Value example that I find most inspiring is the origin story of Airbnb: how Airbnb's founders, Brian Chesky and Joe Gebbia, first tested their business idea.

Facing difficulty paying their rent, they noticed that an upcoming design conference was going to bring a few thousand designers to San Francisco, the city where they lived. They knew that hotel capacity would be limited, and that the rates would be expensive; i.e. conference participants were going to need somewhere to stay (their outcome), but face some obstacles.

So why not create a bed-and-breakfast service in their apartment during the conference? Their apartment was sufficiently large to host a few guests, and they already happened to have three air mattresses stored in the wardrobe.

They prototyped their idea by creating a simple website, including an explanation of how this new service would work. This initial prototyped website included a listing showing three airbeds available in their apartment, at a price of 80 dollars each per night.

It was time to test, especially given that staying in someone else's apartment was not commonplace at that time.

Having promoted their website through some design blogs and the conference organizers, within a few days three guests had booked – all of whom were in the core customer profile that Chesky and Gebbia were aiming for, designers coming to the conference on a budget.

They succeeded in making $1,000 – real-life evidence that their innovative offer idea could provide value for both customers and also for themselves.

Several further rounds of testing and iterative improvement then followed, involving Nathan

Blecharczyk, who had significant software and coding expertise, and became Airbnb's third co-founder. Improvement took place on the idea itself and also the business model.

A second version of the website was tested at South by Southwest, one of the leading tech-industry gatherings, and a third version of the website was tested during the Democratic National Convention, when the founders succeeded in driving so much traffic to the site that it crashed.

And, as they say, the rest is history. At the time of writing, Airbnb has grown to over 5 million hosts who have welcomed over 2 billion guest arrivals in almost every country across the world. A great example of how prototyping, testing and iterating can successfully verify the value of an offer idea.

Actions to accelerate

Here are the top three actions to help you move forward quickly:

1. With your taskforce team, decide how you are going to PROTOTYPE your prioritized offer idea – and then proceed to create it.
2. Decide how best to TEST your prototype – and then proceed to run as many tests as possible, making sure to iteratively IMPROVE your offer idea based on the feedback from your core customers.
3. Repeat the PROTOTYPE – TEST – IMPROVE loop until you're confident that your idea will create sufficient value for both core customers and your company.

10

Step 7:
Achieve the Ambition

A

Remember the story I shared at the beginning of Chapter 7, about new water bottles for kids based on movie characters? Well, that project also taught me some other important lessons about how to innovate successfully.

One day, we were in a taskforce team meeting working on the launch of that product, when someone announced, 'We should sell them in toy stores!'

There was a momentary silence whilst the other team members digested this comment. Intuitively it made perfect sense – after all, these cute little character water bottles were designed for kids and looked like toys. However, there was also some hesitation and reticence given that toy shops didn't typically sell bottles of water, and therefore we didn't have any existing toy shop retail customers.

It was at that moment I realized that I had never truly understood the concept commonly known as 'distribution'. Up until that point, I'd always thought about distribution decisions as being responses to the question 'Where do we want to sell our offer?' Whereas the better question, adopting a more customer-centric approach, would have been 'How can we make it as easy as possible for our core customers to access, and then purchase, our offer?'

As we've seen many times throughout this book, customers should always be top of mind when innovating, and putting ourselves in their shoes will help us identify the best places to sell our offer.

Once we'd decided on all of the various places where it would make sense to sell our new kids' water bottles from a customer perspective, what then? Well, we needed to focus on how we would create and build customer demand.

It's amazing how many people in our organization still believed that if we created something great, it would simply sell itself. In our dreams! Unless our core customer was aware that our new product existed, and had seen or heard relevant and compelling messages about it, then the harsh truth was that we were unlikely to sell very many.

Our work on these two elements – where our core customer would **access** the offer, and how we would **activate** our core customer audience – became our launch plan, and it proved to be a very effective one.

In parallel to these plans being formed, we needed to make this product real and ready for launch: finalizing product design and technical development, as well as preparing for production and logistics at scale. Not always seen as the most glamorous part of an innovation project, but one of the most critical.

As previously mentioned, this product was a commercial success around the world, won several industry awards, and positively impacted kids' drinking habits. I'll never forget receiving a handwritten letter from a mum who had written to our corporate headquarters to thank us for the fact that her son now actively wanted to drink water, whereas he previously only drank soft drinks.

One of my biggest learnings from this project, reinforced many times on other projects since then, is that we are often too inward looking and company-centric when launching. We focus on preparing the rocket and sending it up into space. However, the act of launching a rocket in itself does not guarantee project success. Success is only achieved when the rocket lands safely, at its planned destination, and fully achieves its mission – or, in our case, when our innovative offer creates value for both customers and our company, and achieves the objectives fixed in our frame.

The learnings on this kids' project were at the genesis of the Achieve the Ambition step.

—

Objective

The objective of this Achieve the Ambition step is threefold. First, to define where it is best to sell your new offer to make it as easy as possible for your core customer to access it. Second, to create a plan which excites core customers and triggers them to consider, purchase, use or consume. And, finally, to do everything else required to get your offer out into the world.

Why is this step so important?

There are three key reasons why this step is so important:

✓ It enables you to extract the maximum business value from your new offer. Remember that, up until this point, zero business value has been created in the real world from your project. It is this step which helps you to make the transition from project to successful commercial launch.

✓ Following on from the above point, this step helps to maximize the ROII (return on innovation investment) from all of the hard work, time, money and resources you and your organization have dedicated to developing your innovative offer so far.

Remember that any organization has a myriad of different choices of where it can focus its time and resources, so you have a vested interest in ensuring that every innovative project you lead delivers as strong a payback as possible.

✓ Doing this step well enables you to help the maximum number of core customers with your offer. As I mentioned at the beginning of this book, innovation is really about making people's lives better. Providing a high-quality offer, easy access and exciting activation helps to maximize the scale of your impact on people's lives.

What are the key risks if you skip this step or do it badly?

There are three key risks:

- Your core customers will not know about your new offer, and clearly this is a prerequisite for them to purchase. Whilst this may seem obvious, it can often be overlooked if you've adopted a 'build it and they will come' mentality.

  You have spent days, weeks, months, often years working on this project, and so you know it intimately. However, remember that your core customers do not, and will not unless you find an effective way to share this news with them.

- Even if your core customers become aware of it, they won't know how it will make their life better. People only buy products and services to get some benefits, because there's something in it for them. Awareness alone is never enough.

  In your everyday life, you are aware of many brands, products and services that you would not choose to purchase. You need to move your core customer from being passively aware to being actively motivated to purchase, otherwise you won't achieve your growth goal.

- Your core customers won't be able to find it, or see it's available for purchase – again, a prerequisite for project success. Much of human behaviour, including shopping behaviour, is habitual: we tend to shop in similar places, buying similar products and services.

It can therefore take a disproportionate amount of effort for companies to break that cycle with new offers. Being highly visible and easily accessible at point of purchase, ideally in a way which triggers impulse buying, is a powerful way to achieve this.

Steps to success

Now that you have identified a winning offer for your core customers and your company, in this step, it is time to plan how you will launch it into the world, to undertake all other requirements prior to launch, and then actually launch it! Being rigorous at this stage will help you to extract as much value as possible from all of the hard work and resources you've dedicated to the project so far.

The key power question for this step is:

> **How can we best implement this offer to maximize our probability of success?**

As always, there are three sub-steps to help you do this. Please note that these sub-steps are not sequential: it is often much more efficient to manage these at the same time in parallel, especially as they will typically be led by different members of the taskforce team.

ACCESS

ACTIVATE

ACTUALIZE

ACCESS

Let's think about the following power question:

> **How can we provide the easiest possible access to our new offer for our core customers?**

The best way to answer this question is by thinking about the real-life customer journey of your core customer, focusing on times when they are trying to achieve their outcome, and then identifying relevant distribution points. As mentioned at the beginning of this chapter, this customer-centric approach will be much more powerful than simply defaulting to where you distribute or sell your existing offers, and will be especially helpful in identifying incremental distribution opportunities for growth.

Your key priority here is to create an access plan. This plan will comprise distribution points which may be physical (for example, retail stores) or online (for example, e-commerce retailers) – or, most often, a combination of both.

For example, imagine you have developed an innovative new car which uses sustainable fuel, targeted at young, eco-conscious consumers. You will need to think about their customer journey when choosing and purchasing a car today, and how you can make it as easy as possible for them to buy your innovative new car at various distribution points along that journey.

In addition to the customer journey, it is also useful to look back at your core customer profile (the WHO from Fix the Frame) as this should also provide relevant information, such as where your core customers live, which websites they use most often, and so on.

Returning to the car example above. You may choose to focus your access on a branded direct-to-consumer e-commerce website with high-quality mobile experience, as your young consumer target is a digital native and happy to make even large purchases online.

You may choose to complement this with physical distribution in a small number of car dealerships which specialize in more ecological vehicles, or in geographical areas which overindex with your core customer profile – as your core customers are likely to visit these places to view various car options prior to their online purchase.

Your access plan should not only focus on identifying the individual distribution points but also designing the journey that you would ideally like your core customer to follow between them. In this way, the distribution points can work in synergy together, therefore being more effective in guiding the customer through a seamless purchasing experience.

If you do identify relevant new distribution channels, you do not necessarily have to start from scratch as this can take time, effort and budget. It can often be very effective to team up with another non-competitive company that already has access to that distribution channel. This is win-win: you get access to an incremental distribution channel with limited effort, and your partner is able to service the channel more cost-effectively, thanks to your financial contribution.

Three final important points on ACCESS. First, whatever channels of distribution you decide on, make sure to check that these channels, when combined in your access plan, can deliver sufficient value to achieve the business objectives from your frame.

Remember that whilst some channels may deliver less value, they may bring other benefits such as prestige or visibility.

Second, make sure that the distribution channels you select are financially feasible for your company and your innovation project; i.e. they have a cost structure which is acceptable.

Certain distribution channels can have very high cost of entry and/or very high cost for ongoing distribution, making it very expensive to sell your offer there. These costs may be significant lump sums of investment to 'get in the door' or high profit margin expectations. Make sure you fully understand these costs at this stage, to avoid any nasty financial surprises later on.

Third, make sure to put yourself in the shoes of whomever owns or controls the channels through which you want to sell your offer, and ask the question,

'What's in it for me?' Unless they have sufficient tangible reasons to support or stock your offer, they are unlikely to do so.

Clearly, these reasons will often revolve around them making more money. You can use the growth goals from Step 1 as a way of thinking about this: if they support or stock your new offer, will it help them to get their customers to buy more? To buy more often? To pay more? Or help them to recruit more customers?

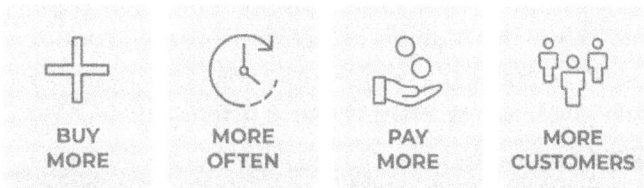

BUY MORE   MORE OFTEN   PAY MORE   MORE CUSTOMERS

Sometimes, it's not just about the money. They might want to re-invigorate *their* offer, or want to boost their perception as an innovator, or even try to convince shareholders about the future of their company. The more deeply you can understand their needs, the better you will be able to position your offer as a solution to help them achieve them.

ACTIVATE

If ACCESS is about building a plan of distribution, then ACTIVATE is about building a plan of communication and influence.

'Activate' may seem like an odd word. Whilst I've never seen an official definition, what I am talking about here is going beyond traditional one-way media, and taking a more active, interactive and experiential approach to drive customer excitement and engagement.

The power question for this is:

How can we truly engage our core customers and inspire them to buy our new offer?

Remember that whilst you and your taskforce team know all about your offer in intricate detail, as it has probably been at the centre of your lives for many months or years, no one knows anything about it yet in the real world, nor why they should care about it.

This ACTIVATE sub-step involves making a smart selection from the huge number of communication and influence levers available to you and creating the most engaging customer experience around the time of launch and also ongoing.

Your activation plan should be built on two core pillars:

1. A single-minded, clear, compelling and creative **message**, which is likely to be a combination of words and images. This pillar is sometimes called the 'creative' or the 'content'.

2. A selection of **media**; i.e. touchpoints where you place your message, which have been specifically chosen to be effective and impactful in reaching your core customer. This pillar is sometimes called 'communication channels'.

   The touchpoints in your activation plan may be digital and online or exist physically in the real world. You will probably use a combination of both, as this is likely to be most effective in getting your message in front of your core customers.

Let's first look at message. I don't have enough space here to provide a full masterclass on how to create high-performing content, communication or advertising, but here are five simple pointers (definitely not rules!) which have proved highly effective for me in the past.

First, your core customers must actually notice the message that you want them to see, which means that it must grab their attention.

In today's world, which is rammed full of messaging, with a huge number of businesses and brands trying to grab people's attention constantly, this is pretty tough. What grabs attention? You might want to start with a large, bold and colourful visual. Research shows that the human brain can identify images far faster than reading text.

Second, you will need a powerful headline of text. As well as grabbing attention, it must also capture your core customers' curiosity and interest.

Headlines need to be short, punchy and ideally shout about the core benefit that your customer will get from buying your innovative offer – in other words, their desired outcome. Resist the temptation to list all of the features of your offer – it is their desired outcome that your core customers are most interested in.

And don't forget to shout about how your offer is different and better than the alternatives.

Third, you ideally want the message to elicit some kind of emotional engagement amongst your core customers.

Think about the adverts that you remember and appreciate most, and I bet that they stirred some kind of emotion in you: whether that was joy, fear or maybe nostalgia. Without emotion, it is highly likely that your message will simply be ignored.

Fourth, you need to give your customer a call-to-action; i.e. you should help them by telling them exactly what to do next if they are interested in getting more information or want to purchase.

This could be as simple as putting a website address, or the logos of retailers where your offer is distributed. This is clearly heavily linked to your access plan; i.e. making it as easy as possible for your core customer to find and purchase your new offer.

Fifth, when developing your message, make sure to test it with your core customers to ensure that it will be effective. Don't trust your own judgement as it is unlikely that you are in the core customer profile.

There are many ways to test messages, from physically showing them to core customers through to testing them online. Online testing can be highly efficient and effective as it enables you to share the message(s) with a high number of your core customers, and get high-quality performance data almost instantly, at very low cost.

Whilst I wouldn't recommend developing messages in a democratic way in a large group, I would actively encourage co-creating and refining messages with a few of your core customers, as this can help maximize both impact and relevance.

If creating a message seems daunting, 'Think, Feel, Do' is a simple framework that you can use to get started. It can be expressed as the following power question:

> **As a result of seeing or hearing our message, what do we want our core customers to think, feel and do?**

Make sure to identify your desired Think, Feel and Do separately, as this will give you the most precision and granularity in the ACTIVATE result you are looking to achieve. This framework ensures that you cover all aspects of successful communication and influence; i.e. the rational (Think), the emotional (Feel) and the desired action (Do).

Now let's look at media. When I started working with media owners back in 1998, it was a pretty simple task. For example, if we wanted to advertise on TV, there were just a handful of TV channels, and the choice was pretty obvious based on the profile of our core customers. Internet advertising was in its infancy, and social media hadn't yet been invented. How different the media landscape is today!

Again, I cannot provide exhaustive guidance here regarding how to create a great media and touchpoint plan, but I want to share two pointers (again, not rules) which have proved effective for me in the past:

First, look back at the core customer profile in your frame, think about their customer journey, and ask the following power questions:

> **What media and touchpoints are our core customers most likely to see?**
>
> **When and where are they most likely to be receptive to our message?**

In terms of media and touchpoints, think about when they are trying to achieve their desired outcome, and also more generally in their everyday life. In terms of when and where they are likely to be receptive to your message, think about when and where they experience the strongest desire for the outcome, or experience the most or largest obstacles.

Second, think widely about all of the various types of media which may be open to you. There are probably many more choices than you think there are. One helpful way in which media types are often classified is following the 'POEMS' acronym (where the 'M' refers to 'Media'):

Paid media: unsurprisingly this refers to media that you pay for. Paid media includes TV advertising, press advertising, radio advertising, outdoor advertising (for example, billboards), and online advertising (for example, Google Ads).

Paid media can also include retail media: the various paid media options which are available at point of purchase, for example in-store display screens and tannoy announcements. Retail media can be highly effective in driving sales, due to its proximity with the point of purchase – and can sometimes bring additional benefits such as additional space in-store through secondary placements.

Owned media: this refers to media over which you have full ownership and control. This includes your company or brand website, your blog, and email newsletters to customers.

This category also includes your company's internal communications channels, which can be very powerful means of amplifying the message about your new offer to employees who can act as ambassadors outside the office walls.

Earned media: this refers to the additional 'organic' exposure and visibility generated as a result of you doing a great job! Earned media can include word-of-mouth, PR, media coverage, journalist mentions and customer reviews.

Social media: historically, social media was classified under Owned media, as companies felt like they had full ownership and control over their social media accounts. However, over time, this has proved to not be completely true – after all, social media companies can effectively make changes to their platforms and algorithms as and when they want.

Whilst social media can be a very effective activation tool, it is not a magic solution. Don't fall into the trap of assuming that 'signing an influencer' will automatically generate a successful sales result.

The more relevant that you are to the real-life context of your core customer, the more effective the activation is likely to be. As a basic example, you could expect that a billboard promoting a health-related offer would probably perform better if it were placed next to a gym, and also if it were placed during a time of year when people are specifically looking to get healthy.

Despite what you might hope, your core customers are unlikely to be ready and waiting whenever you decide to launch, as they already have many other things happening in their lives. So you will probably need to work much harder than you think to drive awareness and convince them that your offer will indeed make their lives better.

So think about how you can execute your plans in as big, bold and brilliant a way as possible. Think about how you can maximize the total amount of budget, energy and effort you can put behind them, to maximize your ROII.

ACTUALIZE

This is the critical time when you get all final elements of your offer ready to launch – and then actually launch! This is the critical time when your innovative offer starts to create tangible value for your customers and your company in the real world.

The power question for this sub-step is:

> **What else needs to be done**
> **to transform our innovative offer into**
> **a customer and commercial success?**

Depending on your industry, and the type of offer that you are launching, there can be many diverse actions required at this stage, but common ones include:

⇒ Briefing the sales team to give them advance notice that your new offer is coming, as well as preparing the key materials they will need to sell it.

⇒ Finalizing design; i.e. what your offer looks like, and how it works, including designing any elements of packaging that may be required, and also testing these.

⇒ Finalizing technical development and specifications; i.e. how the offer will be delivered from a technical perspective, and making sure this is fully tested.

⇒ Finalizing industrialization; i.e. how your offer will be produced at scale. This is typically more complex for physical products than it is for digital services.

⇒ Finalizing testing with customers, especially if additional reassurance or validation is required for stakeholder approval.

⇒ Finalizing the financials, especially the profit and loss (P&L). Cost of goods is very important here; i.e. how much it will cost your company to produce the offer.

⇒ Finalizing pricing. As well as customer willingness to pay, also be sure to bear in mind your access plan (i.e. where you are going to sell it), the competitive context (i.e. how many alternatives there are to your offer, how good they are, and how they are priced), and the strength of your company or brand – not forgetting how much your offer will cost you to produce and sell.

⇒ Finalizing the volume, revenue and margin commitments and forecasts – notably how many of your offer you are going to sell and how much money you are going to make – making sure to explicitly compare this to the frame you fixed in Step 1.

⇒ Finalizing any required elements regarding intellectual property (IP), especially if there are some elements of your innovative offer that are truly unique to you, that you might want to protect.

⇒ Finalizing a risk assessment; i.e. what are the most likely things that could go wrong, and how can you mitigate them.

It is especially important to be vigilant about competitors. What your competitors were offering when you started to work on this innovation project might be quite different in terms of what they are offering now – either in their offers and/or their pricing. It is important that you have an up-to-date vision of this pre-launch.

⇒ Executing the ACCESS and ACTIVATE plans that you drafted above, to ensure that your core customers can not only find your offer easily, but are also highly motivated to purchase.

⇒ Building the awareness and engagement plan for other key stakeholder groups, including distribution partners, sales reps and retail colleagues.

Whilst it can seem like an additional 'nice-to-have', make sure to create a strong internal activation campaign – not only to get the company excited about the launch of this new offer, but also recruit them as informal ambassadors to drive visibility and desire amongst their network.

Of course, it is still possible that some projects will be killed off at this late phase. This could be due to the lack of a technical solution, insufficient quality, unsatisfactory P&L, or a change of priorities within the company. If this happens, don't just stop the project and walk away – go straight to Step 10, Reflect and Review and capture project learnings, which will help to maximize probability of success on your next innovation project.

Top tips

✓ If you have any questions or doubts about your offer at this step, or any key decisions to make, get your core customers to guide you towards the best solution. It is much better to do this than to make assumptions, as this can inject unhelpful risk into your project.

✓ Whilst you are creating your ACTIVATE plans, and the associated budgets, it is important to remember that you should not stop activating directly after the initial launch campaign. Rather, you must plan to continue to activate over time. Think of this like building a relationship. You can't build a strong relationship in a one-shot big bang – you need to continue to nurture it over time to build strong foundations.

I remember seeing a proprietary in-depth quantitative research study some years ago which showed a direct correlation between the success of an offer in-market and its activation. The conclusion of this research: the business performance of offers is only fully maximized if they are regularly supported by activation during the first two years after launch.

So make sure that this is anticipated in your activation plans (and budgets) from the start, to maximize the financial return from your offer.

Lessons from leaders

The brand which immediately springs to mind as best-in-class at the Achieve the Ambition step is the energy drink Red Bull. Red Bull was highly innovative with both its access and activation plans at launch, both of which were critical factors in its success.

In terms of access: instead of defaulting to where beverage companies normally distributed their products, they adopted much more of a customer-centric approach. They were guided by places frequented by their core customers, especially places where they needed an energy boost.

This led to Red Bull prioritizing non-traditional distribution channels for a soft drink, such as nightclubs and bars, music events and gyms, rather than mass-market supermarkets.

Knowing that students often needed an energy boost, Red Bull also focused on providing easy access to the product on college campuses. This was amplified by its Student Marketeer programme, where college students promoted the drink on campus and organized exciting events.

Not only did this access approach allow its core customers to get easy access to the product, but it also contributed to the 'coolness' and differentiation of the brand vs. other more ubiquitous beverage brands.

Red Bull's activation approach at launch was a masterclass in how to inspire and delight customers and remains so today. It pioneered high-performance live events and content marketing as core activation strategies.

The brand created and sponsored extreme sports contests: for example, the Red Bull Flugtag (German for 'flight day'), known as 'the world's wackiest air-show'. This is a competition in which teams of everyday people design, build and launch human-powered flying contraptions off a ramp into a body of water.

Needless to say that flying elephants, gliding hamburgers and pianos with wings easily capture customer attention and interest in the brand.

Or who can forget the Red Bull Stratos project which captured the world's attention in 2012: one of the first moments of global virality in the digital age. Felix Baumgartner jumped from a capsule nearly 40 km above the New Mexico desert, plunged at a top speed of 1,357.6 kph and broke three world records in the process: the highest freefall, highest crewed balloon flight and first person to travel faster than the speed of sound in freefall. All nicely branded Red Bull, of course.

Beyond the inventiveness of such experiential activation, the rich media content and coverage of such unorthodox, edgy events is unparalleled, serving as Red Bull advertising, fuelling brand buzz and boosting customer desire.

Actions to accelerate

Here are the top three actions to help you move forward quickly:

1. With your taskforce team, build a master plan for all of the actions required at this step.
2. Assign who is going to be responsible to make each one of these actions happen, and in what timings.
3. Specifically agree how you are going to work and communicate together as a taskforce team over this period, to ensure that plans remain coherent,

synergies between the different workstreams are maximized, and any risks are shared and mitigated.

Given how much work you have put into this project so far, make sure to enjoy and celebrate the launch when you get there!

11

Step 8: Track the Traction

T

The innovative offer had just been launched onto the market. After 18 months of hard graft, the taskforce team was visibly relieved to have got to this stage. I bumped into the Marketing Director responsible for the project in the corridor of global headquarters and asked her how the product was performing so far. Her response was 'Unfortunately we now need to wait about three months to get the first batch of in-market retail data'.

I found this response both surprising and, quite frankly, disappointing. After all, if you are passionate about your innovation, you cannot wait a few months without getting feedback.

I was fully aware that there can sometimes be a time lag before receiving market data – at least this was the case back in those days. But did this mean that the taskforce team should simply sit back and do nothing until that data landed on their desks? Absolutely not!

Here are the two key pieces of advice I shared with the Marketing Director that day to help her move her project forward in a strong way:

First, information about the performance of the new offer can, and should, be gathered from Day 1 post-launch. The taskforce team should have already anticipated this and have planned to spend a significant amount of time out of the office.

For example, for a product launch, you might head into retail stores to observe and ask questions to core customers, ask store staff how well the product is selling so far, or accompany sales reps to see the degree to which shelves have been shopped.

Alternatively, you may choose to mobilize company employees to lead a product sampling campaign in high-footfall locations with a high quantity of your core customers, capturing feedback via a short and simple questionnaire.

Other opportunities might include using social media to ask first customers to share their experiences or creating a poll for customers to vote for their favourite product in the new range.

There are many options available to you to capture this initial feedback. However you choose to do this, be assured that no knowledge of research or innovation metrics is required, but simply the curiosity to go and find out what is going on. Clearly, a large proportion of this initial feedback may be qualitative and with a relatively small sample size, but this does not detract from its value.

Second, of course, it will be necessary to also capture performance in more formal ways with more formal metrics. Whilst it can sometimes be tempting to measure many diverse metrics on an innovation project – a situation sometimes driven by standard process, governance or indeed the whims of specific stakeholders – I strongly recommend tracking as few metrics as possible to drive focus and clarity in the analysis.

Ensure that these metrics are as laser-focused and aligned as possible to the project objectives you identified when you fixed the frame, including the growth goal. Try to ensure that the metrics you track are as closely aligned as possible to those being tracked at a company or brand level, for instance revenue or turnover, to ensure that the contribution of the project to overall business performance is easily visible.

Collecting information and data is one thing. Understanding it and effectively communicating it is another. Make sure to avoid the so-called stakeholder expectation gap where your stakeholders' expectations of receiving news about your project's progress do not match what you actually communicate. Generally speaking, within large organizations, no news is automatically interpreted as bad news – and, especially in today's short-termist business cultures which lack patience, good news is required to be shared quickly.

My discussion with this Marketing Director was at the genesis of the Track the Traction step.

—

Objective

The objective of this Track the Traction step is therefore to get initial customer feedback, as well as a quantitative and qualitative understanding of whether you are achieving the goals that you fixed in your frame at the beginning of the project. We do this by proactively sourcing real-life data about how the offer is performing – both immediately after launch and ongoing.

Why is this step so important?

There are three key reasons why this step is so important:

✓ It forces you to remain connected to the reality of your core customers, and their behaviour.

As we've seen from the very beginning of this book, customer-centricity is a key factor for successful innovation, and this also involves the period post-launch. It's critical to keep as close an eye as possible on whether your core customers are buying, using or consuming – and, if so, where, when and how much.

Over time, it is also critical to monitor what level of repeat purchase there is, as this can be a strong indicator of whether or not your offer delivered against their needs.

It's also important to capture if your core customers are *not* purchasing, using or consuming and, in that case, to try to understand why not. In some cases, there may be a quick fix that you can make: for example, sharpening a key message within your activation.

✓ It will enable you to measure how you are progressing vs. the objectives and metrics that you set when you fixed the frame, right at the beginning of your innovation project.

Remember that innovation is only a means to achieving a goal, so you need to ensure that you can see whether you are on track to achieve that goal. This is especially important for successful stakeholder management, as it minimizes the risk of stakeholders forming their own subjective opinion of whether the offer is performing.

✓ This step will enable you to identify what can be optimized in the next step, Optimize the Offer. Clearly any changes you will make to improve your offer should be based on real-life data and evidence, rather than opinion or feeling.

What are the key risks if you skip this step or do it badly?

There are three key risks:

• You will be unclear about how your project is performing, what customers are thinking and doing, and therefore whether any corrective action may be required.

Without evidence or data, it is like trying to walk somewhere blindfolded: you may be making progress towards your destination, or indeed moving in the opposite direction from your destination, but overall you are less likely to succeed.

• In the absence of seeing any evidence or data, your internal stakeholders are highly likely to speculate and create their own subjective opinion about project performance, and this is likely to be negative.

It is really important for you to control the narrative with real-life project performance information, data and evidence. A proactive approach here also demonstrates that you are still leading and fully in control of the project and haven't taken your foot off the gas during this critical post-launch period.

- You may miss opportunities to capitalize on good news. Positive customer reviews, positive retailer testimonials, any positive press or media coverage, or reports of stores selling out of stock, can all be used as proof points that your new offer is performing well, which can further boost its visibility and distribution – after all, everyone loves to back a winner.

Steps to success

In this step, you will gather evidence to answer the following three power questions:

What evidence is there that our core customers positively value our new offer?

What evidence is there that suggests that our core customers may not appreciate our new offer, or certain elements of it?

What evidence is surprising vs. our expectations?

To quickly expand a bit on that last power question. It is quite possible that you will have some surprises after your offer hits the market.

For example, up until now, you've been focusing on one core customer profile, but maybe now you discover that your offer also appeals to another customer profile. This is important to know, as it may represent an additional growth opportunity.

Or maybe your core customers are using or consuming your offer in a way that you didn't expect. This may help you to refine your message, to further drive its effectiveness.

As always, there are three sub-steps to help you with this:

COMPILE

ANALYSE

CONCLUDE

COMPILE

Your first sub-step here is a basic one: that of compiling as much different evidence, data and information as possible to help your understanding about offer performance.

The power question here is:

> **What are all of the different sources of evidence and data we can get to help us understand what is happening?**

Basic, yes, but not always so simple. There are likely to be many different sources of data and evidence – both from inside your company (for example, how much of your offer you have sold), and from outside (for example, how much your offer is being used or consumed, or how much it is appreciated by customers). Your behaviour here should be full curiosity with a fully open mind. Try not to have a mental filter where you only look for positive evidence which shows what a great job you have done, as otherwise you are highly likely to miss any potential problems.

Make sure to look at both quantitative and qualitative evidence and data. Quantitative evidence is likely to revolve around how much you have sold, how much has been consumed/used, how many places it is being distributed and so on. Qualitative data may include feedback via the sales force, online customer reviews or customer feedback on social media. The key is to get your hands on as much evidence as possible.

Especially for the quantitative data, it can be very helpful to have some benchmarks, to put the numbers from your offer into context vs. the numbers for similar offers. It is very difficult to understand whether your new offer is truly performing well or badly without this context.

If you are selling a digital offer, especially if you are selling it directly to customers, you are very likely to have access to all sales data immediately and in real time. This is extremely valuable, especially as it will also allow you to immediately know the impact of any optimizations you make to your offer in the next step.

Be wary of your own internal sales data if you sell to an intermediary such as a retailer or a distributor. Especially at launch, just because you may have sold and shipped lots of volume does not provide any evidence that your core customers are actually buying it.

If you are selling your offer through large distributors or retailers, they often have databases based on their loyalty card, which enable you to get a granular understanding of which customer profiles are buying, when and where they are buying, how often they are buying, whether customers are re-purchasing and so on. You will probably need to pay for access to this data, but it is highly valuable.

These databases can also often tell you what your new offer is being purchased with – another highly valuable piece of information which can be leveraged to create joint activation or cross-selling deals.

Observation can also be a very powerful tool as part of this COMPILE sub-step. Try to observe your core customers in two specific instances:

First, when and where they are considering purchasing an offer which delivers the same outcome as your new offer. For example, imagine that you have launched an innovative new cleaning product. (With the right permissions, of course), head into relevant retail outlets to observe customers shopping in the cleaning aisle: do they notice your product on the shelf or walk straight past it? Do they hesitate when they see it, or pick it up to have a closer look? Do they purchase it? If so, how many? What other types of products were they buying at the same time?

Second, ideally you will also observe some customers who have already purchased your offer, whilst they are using or consuming it. In the case of the cleaning product: do they read the instructions or know intuitively how to use it? In which room of the house did they use it? Did it actually get the cleaning result they wanted? How much of the product did they use? Where did they store the product afterwards?

As mentioned in Step 2, Immerse and Inquire, try to observe customers as if through a child's eyes, which means with a high level of curiosity and with no judgement. Try to let your customers do what they would naturally do, without intervening, as this is the way in which you will get the richest and most accurate learnings.

Once you have completed your observation and understand what your core customers are doing with regards to your new offer, try to go more deeply beneath the surface to understand *why*. You can do this through questioning, asking as many open questions as possible to get the richest possible understanding – as close to the time and place where they interacted with your offer.

We often think that we're bothering people when we ask for their opinion on new offers. But the reality is that people are often flattered to be asked: after all, if you ask their opinion, it means that you value their opinion, which is a positive thing. Ask open questions which are most likely to provide clear indications of whether they value your new offer or not, and why or why not. And feel free to use my favourite question: 'How could we make this offer a 10 out of 10 for you?'

Whatever you see or hear, remember not to be judgemental. There are always reasons why people do what they do, and say what they say, even though it might seem strange to you. Make the effort to try to understand things from your core customers' perspective, not your own.

Once you've compiled as much evidence as possible, it's time to move on to the next sub-step.

ANALYSE

Unsurprisingly, the heart of this sub-step is analysis – trying to make sense of all the various evidence and data you have just collected.

The key power question to guide you here is:

> **Based on the evidence and data,**
> **what are our core customers actually doing**
> **with regards to our new offer and why?**

Two important points here: (1) make sure to do this analysis for both the buyer and the beneficiary, where relevant; and (2) in your analysis, make sure to cover both purchase and usage/consumption.

The amount of time and effort required here will depend on how much evidence and data you have been able to gather. However much you have, the guiding principle stays the same. Look for two key things: (1) the big themes which can be built by connecting multiple bits of evidence and data; and (2) any weak signals which are currently visible at a low level, but are potentially early signs of something which could have a significant or negative impact in the future.

Whilst your analysis will probably consist of several pages or slides, force yourself to write a one-page summary. This can be a tough exercise, but it will help you to prioritize those elements of the analysis that are truly important vs. those that may be more anecdotal.

And, when you're preparing your analysis, make sure that you put yourself in the shoes of the stakeholders that you will be sharing it with. Let's be clear: nobody wants to look at a spreadsheet full of numbers.

Build a simple, clear and compelling narrative from the data and evidence you have compiled and then use that data and evidence to illustrate your key messages. It might be helpful to build this narrative based on the following four points:

1. Here's a reminder of the frame, and the innovation insight.
2. Here's a reminder of the offer we launched, including where, when and how.
3. Here's an overview of the different sources of evidence and data we compiled.
4. Here are the key conclusions made by the taskforce team.

Make sure that this analysis is as visual as possible – for example, with graphs and photos – as this can help your audience to understand the key messages much more quickly and easily.

CONCLUDE

Now you have prepared your analysis, it is time to share it with relevant stakeholders and ensure that there is full alignment on the conclusions.

The key power questions to guide you here are:

> **Do we all agree on the key conclusions from the analysis?**
>
> **And, if not, why not?**

Where possible, make this a plenary discussion with all key stakeholders together, ideally in person. This typically allows for more effective discussion and debate than an online meeting, or individual check-ins with individual stakeholders.

The only output that's required at this sub-step is alignment; i.e. all key stakeholders share the same vision of what has been learned about the performance of your offer so far. Of course, this performance should be considered in the context of your frame.

This explicit alignment is critical before any optimization actions can be taken in the next step.

Top tips

✓ When you're observing and questioning your core customers, try to record as much of this as possible, with their permission of course. Video footage filmed on mobile is best, but photos and audio are also helpful if video is not possible. This material can be very powerful indeed for illustrating key data points to stakeholders.

✓ Empower the front line. Your sales, service and support teams are likely to hear customer feedback first. So, make it super easy for them to share this feedback with you, and don't hesitate to recognize and reward them when they share high-quality feedback to demonstrate its usefulness.

✓ If possible, pre-circulate the analysis before the stakeholder discussion – ideally a week beforehand, to give them enough time to read it. Not only does this show that you are on the front foot with your analysis, but it also allows them to contact you before the discussion if they have any specific questions or concerns.

Learnings from leaders

New technologies now enable companies to track customer feedback much more quickly and easily than ever before, and Unilever is a great example of a company embracing this, with their initiative called Digital Voice of the Consumer (DVOC).

Their first step is to tap into millions of pieces of publicly available feedback data from consumer ratings and reviews that are published on different websites across their markets. They then process this data to group it into topics, using artificial intelligence to recognize certain terms and identify common themes.

After that, this material is used by cross-functional teams to create superior products and deliver better consumer experiences. The teams work together to prioritize any changes they might want to make to existing products, as well as identifying insights that can help shape innovative projects for the future.

Importantly, Unilever recognizes the importance of a proactive posture here to gather the feedback that's publicly available, as many consumers may not reach out to them directly.

This approach has had a major positive business impact. In terms of optimizing products, they were able to address leakage issues identified on home care products in China by redesigning the packaging. In terms of new products, examples include successfully launching a new variant of Domestos in Turkey thanks to consumer demand.

This kind of approach allows Unilever to understand fast, react fast and remain consumer-centric – exactly the spirit of Track the Traction, and the step we'll see next, Optimize the Offer.

Actions to accelerate

Here are the top three actions to help you move forward quickly:

1. Anticipate as early as possible that you will need to do this Track the Traction activity to ensure that time is fully blocked in diaries. This is much better than feeling like it is on top of your workload after the launch of your new offer and will help to ensure it doesn't get deprioritized by other day-to-day issues.

2. Already book your CONCLUDE meeting with stakeholders into diaries for after the launch. This reassures stakeholders that you will not only do the post-launch analysis, but will also proactively share learnings with them, which builds confidence.

3. Before launch, make sure to pre-identify the different sources of data and evidence you will be able to COMPILE. This will allow you to move more quickly post-launch, and will also help you to pre-empt any data gaps you may have, enabling you to fix these pre-launch.

12

Step 9: Optimize the Offer

Towards the beginning of my career, I was lucky enough to secure the job that I dreamed of as a kid: that of being responsible for Christmas and Easter chocolates for a world-class chocolate manufacturer. What better job can there be than creating presents to be given as gifts, during two major celebration moments for family and friends?

Whilst, obviously, it wasn't *exactly* like Willy Wonka, I was indeed based in a chocolate factory, where delicious chocolate aromas greeted us every morning from the moment that we drove through the factory gate. The quality checking procedure involved someone bringing fresh chocolate from the morning's production up to the office for tasting at precisely 11 o'clock every morning. Whilst not wanting to make you hungry, my favourite was always Twix – soft warm doughy cookie, smooth liquid caramel, and melt-in-the-mouth chocolate. Anyway...

The part of the business I was responsible for was unique as 100% of my product range was seasonal; i.e. there were no products available year-round. There were simply two 'seasons' – the Christmas season and the Easter season. For each of these seasons, I would design and develop a range of around 30 chocolate products. Some of these products would be repeated from the previous season, whilst some of them would be completely new.

This seasonal way of working forced me to ask a very valuable question twice per year: 'What can we do to optimize our offer?', as clearly my objective was to improve business performance year after year.

So, twice a year, I would Track the Traction and analyse the performance of every single product in the range. How did it perform from a business perspective? What customer feedback did we receive, both positive and maybe less positive? Is this in line with what customers want and need right now? Are there customer needs that we are not yet responding to? How difficult was it to sell to our retail partners, and what level of distribution did they give it within retail stores? How did it look on-shelf? What similar products did our competitors launch last season, and how might that influence what we do?

And based on this, twice per year, I would take concrete action to make my offer better: sometimes small tweaks, sometimes major overhauls. Unsurprisingly, this approach systematically led to a better business performance of our seasonal chocolate ranges, year after year.

This experience taught me a very valuable lesson: that you should frequently and consistently be looking to find ways to improve your offer. Adopting a mindset of continuous improvement was at the genesis of this Optimize the Offer step.

This philosophy has also proved incredibly powerful for me since then, in terms of leading Innovinco® to success. When I founded the company, we started out with a long list of 39 services, all of which were given catchy names and logos, and proudly displayed on our website. Each of these services was relevant to our core corporate customers, with a clearly defined customer outcome, and we started selling them very quickly. However, over time, analysis showed that the complexity of our offer was just too overwhelming (including for my small team at that time!).

Fast forward eight years, with the benefit of having frequently and consistently optimized our offer over that time, we made the bold decision to prioritize just a small number of products and services, including our signature INNOVATOR Champions® learning programme. In our specific situation, offer optimization primarily meant focus to achieve world-class excellence; for your business, it will be different.

This optimized offer has led to an optimized business performance, through generating greater customer and company value. At the time of writing, business leaders and managers from over 40 countries have participated in the INNOVATOR Champions®

programme, with 100% of participants feeling more confident in their capability to innovate as a result. The Optimize the Offer approach works!

—

Objective

The objective of this Optimize the Offer step is therefore to further improve and enhance the offer you have launched, such that it adds an increasing amount of value to your customers and your company over time.

Why is this step so important?

There are three key reasons why this step is so important:

✓ It encourages you to acknowledge that, despite how long you may have spent developing it, and how great you may think it is, offers can often be improved. This includes improvements that may be required to respond to a dynamic market, new trends, or even new customer needs.
 Offers should be seen as living organisms rather than static, inert or fixed over time. Once you have acknowledged this, it puts you in the right mindset to actively want to seek out what you can do to make your offers better.
✓ A more valuable offer for your customer is likely to equate to a more valuable offer for your company. So, if you take the time and effort to

optimize your offer over time, you are likely to see a corresponding uplift in business performance. This is very much the same spirit as digital start-ups who are constantly iterating and tweaking their offers and, as a result, are constantly making them better and better, and more valuable. This same spirit also applies to physical products, albeit optimizations can be a bit more complex to implement, often requiring more time and budget.

✓ This approach will help you ensure that your offer remains relevant and therefore delivers value over a longer period of time. The context around your customers will change over time, and therefore it is important that your offer continues to adapt to these changes, if you want it to continue to deliver value for your company.

What are the key risks if you skip this step or do it badly?

There are two key risks:

- You lose the opportunity to fully capitalize on the real-life feedback provided by customers post-launch.
  This can manifest itself in two main ways: either not capitalizing on the elements which are bringing them the most value, or not correcting any aspects which are not fully delivering against their needs or expectations. For the beneficiary, this may be related to their experience of using or

consuming your offer. For the buyer, this may be related to how easy or enjoyable it is to purchase.

- There is a competitive risk. As soon as you launch a new offer onto the market, it is in the public domain, and you can be pretty confident that your competitors will not only see it, but will also be closely scrutinizing it.

They may choose to copy some key elements of your offer through launching a copycat – and, if they have a strong brand or fan base, this may result in success for them, and steal some share of your business. At worst, they will proactively improve your offer and launch a 'topcat', potentially condemning your offer to irrelevancy.

Steps to success

In this step, you will concentrate on the following power question:

> **What will we do to make this offer even more valuable to customers and the company?**

As always, there are three sub-steps to help you do this:

EXPLORE   PRIORITIZE   IMPLEMENT

The spirit of these sub-steps is similar to Step 5, Open up Options, in that you will be exploring multiple possibilities, before prioritizing the most valuable and relevant ones to take forward.

EXPLORE

The starting point here is your summary of conclusions from the previous step, making sure that all cross-functional taskforce team members have the same level of understanding of the data and analysis. Once this is done, the power question which guides this sub-step is:

Based on our Track the Traction conclusions, what potential actions might we take?

Whilst some optimizations may be obvious based on your analysis, it is important to keep an open mind and explore a wide range of potential actions here, to ensure that the most valuable actions are identified.

So, with your taskforce team, generate a long list of potential actions. To help with this, I recommend using a brainstorming approach like we saw in the DIVERGE sub-step of Step 5, Open up Options. No idea is a bad idea, on the condition that it responds directly to the learnings from Track the Traction. Do this on sticky notes, with one optimization idea on each sticky note, to enable easier prioritization later on.

Make sure to sufficiently explore the two angles of optimization: customer and company. On the customer side, think about how your offer could help them achieve their desired outcome more easily, and/or reduce or remove some obstacles which may still exist.

On the company side, take the time to explore what could be optimized from an operational, logistical or financial perspective, focusing on efficiencies – without introducing any risk to customer satisfaction, of course.

PRIORITIZE

Once you have your long list, it is time to prioritize those optimization actions that you will actually implement. Focus on those that will create the maximum value.

I recommend to prioritize them using the same approach as in the CONVERGE sub-step of Step 5, Open up Options; i.e. the Attractive/ Accessible matrix. The only difference being that, this time, Attractive refers to both core customers and your company.

The power questions that can help you with this are as follows. First, for Attractive:

How attractive would this optimization be to our core customer?

To what degree would this optimization help them to achieve their key outcome and remove their key obstacle(s)?

To what degree do we believe that our core customer would be willing to pay extra for this optimization?

To what degree would this optimization generate value and profit for our company?

In an ideal world, you would evaluate the customer-related optimizations with the involvement of real core customers, to bring more robustness and rigour to the prioritization.

Second, for Accessible:

How accessible or feasible would this optimization be for our company to implement?

To what degree would this optimization leverage our company's existing assets, knowledge, capability or infrastructure?

To what degree do we estimate that this optimization would require an acceptable level of investment for the company?

Transfer your optimization ideas to the corresponding position on the Attractive/Accessible matrix, after discussion and alignment with your taskforce team. Those ideas which are placed in the top right-hand quadrant (i.e. perceived as both highly Attractive and Accessible) should be prioritized, as these are the ones which should enable you to deliver greatest value to customers and the company in the easiest way.

Important to note: when deciding which optimizations to prioritize for implementation, there is a balance to strike in terms of effort vs. reward. Given that the resources in a company – financial and human – are typically fixed, it is important to know when the time and effort spent optimizing an offer would be better spent on working on a new innovation project which would create even greater value.

To paraphrase Voltaire, 'Perfection is the enemy of progress'.

IMPLEMENT

Once you have prioritized which optimizations to take forward, it is time to implement them. Some optimizations may be quick wins (or indeed quick corrections, if the optimization resolves a problem), whilst others might take much longer and, for example, may be scheduled over the next 6, 12 or 24 months.

The important thing is to build an implementation plan with the prioritized optimization actions, with time horizons. Align this with key stakeholders and use it to pilot and communicate progress over time. You can use the following power question to guide this:

> What is the optimal roadmap for implementing key optimizations?

Hopefully it goes without saying that, once implemented, the optimizations should be monitored to ensure that they deliver the desired results against the analysis from Track the Traction – both for customers and the company.

Top tips

✓ When exploring possibilities for optimization, make sure to look beyond your offer itself and how you might further boost its performance. For example, could you build new partnerships to help increase access or the level of activation? Could you add a new service around your offer to boost value?

✓ Whilst your core focus will inevitably be on your own offer, make sure to continue to monitor competitors and alternative solutions. They will also continue to evolve after your launch, and may force you to adapt your optimization roadmap.

✓ When you implement an optimization, make sure that this is well communicated both internally and externally. Communicating to customers is especially important here to bring new news, reinforce the value of your offer, and drive increased purchase, consumption or usage.

Learnings from leaders

Whilst this now seems hard to believe, Netflix originally started life as a DVD rental-by-mail service, and has consistently demonstrated Optimize the Offer attitude and behaviour since then.

Its first major optimization was that of capitalizing on the advance in internet technology as a means of delivering Netflix's offer via online streaming. This optimization made it quicker, cheaper and more convenient for customers to access a wide range of movies whenever and wherever they wanted – and also easier for Netflix to provide this access.

Two notable optimizations to their offer since then have included:

• Netflix Originals: content that is produced, co-produced, or distributed exclusively by Netflix.

Many of these 'originals' have enjoyed significant international success.

- Customized thumbnail images: Netflix selects specific designs for a thumbnail based on a customer's viewing history, such as actors, scene or genre preferences. All powered by advanced algorithms and AI, of course. That's right, even within the same household, you will be presented with different thumbnail images for Netflix shows, specifically designed to encourage *you* to watch.

Importantly, these optimizations are fully in line with their mission: 'We are here to entertain the world, one fan at a time'. Even more importantly, Netflix's optimizations have been built from detailed analysis of its customers' preferences.

At the time of writing, Netflix entertains over half a billion people in more than 190 countries and 50 languages. Reed Hastings, Netflix's co-founder, attributes at least some of this success to their inventive, fast and flexible organization. These innovation culture elements are prerequisites for mastering the Optimize the Offer step.

Actions to accelerate

Here are the top three actions to help you move forward quickly:

1. Schedule an EXPLORE and PRIORITIZE session with your taskforce team. Ideally this would have been scheduled as part of the project timeline pre-launch, so it doesn't feel like an additional commitment in diaries post-launch.

2. Before the end of the session, agree who is specifically going to do what to IMPLEMENT the optimizations that you have prioritized, including any stakeholder management or formal project management actions which may be required within your organization.

3. As the optimizations are implemented, remember to monitor how the offer performs. And, of course, you can continue to optimize it as new learnings emerge.

    The iterative Track the Traction ⇔ Optimize the Offer loop should continue until further improvements no longer justify the time, effort or resources required – or when those resources would generate greater returns elsewhere.

13

Step 10:
Reflect and Review

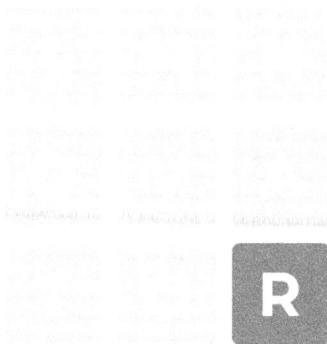

R

'We were so glad to finally get the project finished, we didn't spend much time on that'

'We just sent the template round on email and asked each team member to add a bit'

'The project review documents are stored in a folder on my computer desktop'

'We've all moved onto different projects now, and so are too busy'

I frequently hear these kinds of responses whenever I ask about how project learnings are gathered and shared – yes, even in some of the world's leading companies. Surprising, certainly, but also very common. And, even when project reviews are done, and done well, they are often given very little airtime within the organization – I once heard of '1-minute project debriefs' happening in one company.

Having led many long and often complex innovation projects, I get it. Your primary project focus was to get to project launch, and to get to that point was probably exhausting. You need a break. You want to move on to the next thing as quickly as possible – especially as it's likely to be a sexy new innovative project which you can't wait to get your teeth stuck into.

This review stage can be particularly frustrating if your project has got caught up in some kind of politics: for example, if one senior stakeholder wants to bury the debrief, because it doesn't suit their personal agenda or might negatively affect their future career aspirations. Sadly, a very common scenario.

However, reviewing projects poorly is a massive mistake. Why? Well, whilst the learnings might not bring much value to the innovation project you've just launched, they have the potential to positively benefit every other innovation project that your organization will work on in the future.

It is a bit like a savings account at the bank. With every project, the learnings are like interest, compounding over time, thereby bringing an ever-increasing amount of value and wisdom to the organization about how to successfully innovate. This builds an innovation learning culture, where each innovator's performance, and also the company's innovation performance, increases exponentially over time.

But you must bank the learnings, before you can start benefiting from the interest.

This is the step where it helps to adopt what Carol Dweck, the American psychologist, famously described as a 'growth mindset' – where failure is a learning experience, with mistakes viewed as part of the learning process, not as evidence of incompetence. Where criticism and feedback are constructive and used for growth rather than taken personally.

What types of learnings to capture? Focus your time and energy on capturing what was done, how it was done, what happened, what worked well, and what worked less well. Unless you can openly talk about what did not work, you cannot improve. It is also important to include what you would recommend doing differently to succeed on future projects. This ensures that the learnings are as action-oriented as possible.

Capturing learnings is important. However, to get the benefits described above, learnings must also be shared in an effective way, otherwise this significantly lowers the positive impact that they can bring to the wider organization. First, I recommend focusing on identifying those key people in your organization who are most likely to benefit from your learnings, both now and in the future. And second, I recommend ensuring that they know that these learnings exist, and how they can easily access them as and when they may want to.

In addition to just making the learnings available, I always recommend at least one in-person project review presentation to key stakeholders and peers, involving each member of the taskforce team to ensure a fully cross-functional perspective. There is huge value in people hearing these learnings live and first-hand, as they are more likely to remember them, and therefore pass them on to future project leaders. Such presentations also allow for interactive question and answer sessions, which help to further interrogate and sharpen the learnings gained.

I once had the pleasure of working for a company who were best-in-class at all of the above. Not only documenting every element of every project in a systematic way, but also presenting learnings formally, at multiple time horizons post-launch, and then making this information easily accessible to relevant people via an online project management system. Not surprising then that this company rarely made the same mistake twice, and consistently experienced strong in-market performance. This best-in-class way of working was at the genesis of the Reflect and Review step.

—

Objective

The objective of this Reflect and Review step is therefore to formally capture key learnings about your innovation project and widely share these with relevant people within the organization. These learnings help to build an increasingly high innovation performance within your organization.

Why is this step so important?

There are three key reasons why this step is so important:

✓ It enables leaders of future innovative projects to easily identify and capitalize on the specific factors which worked well with your project, thereby maximizing the probability of success in their project. Imagine how much it would help you to have at your disposal a checklist of key success factors, which not only help to move a project forward, but also do so with more confidence.

✓ Conversely, it helps leaders of future innovative projects to avoid replicating mistakes that have previously been made, thereby reducing risk of failure on their project. Again, imagine how much it would help you to have at your disposal a checklist of key project risks to avoid, based on where previous company initiatives struggled. I think of it as being like a satnav which provides early warning of incidents which may derail your journey, so that you can achieve your destination by taking a better route.

✓ Doing this step helps to build innovator skills – at an individual level initially, and ultimately across the whole organization. The level of skills you have in any domain tends to be directly aligned with the level of performance. Therefore more highly skilled innovators mean higher innovation success, which is obviously the holy grail for many organizations today.

What are the key risks if you skip this step or do it badly?

There are two key risks:

- Your organization's innovation performance will be dependent on the knowledge and capability of a few specific individuals. Knowledge and capability which immediately disappear if these individuals move role or leave the company. All organizations should be aiming to build up innovation knowledge, capabilities and collective intelligence at a company level, based on experience built up over decades.

  Expressed another way, the performance of innovative projects should ideally not be variable depending on the level of knowledge and capability of the specific project leader or taskforce team members. People move between roles and functions frequently; this is part of corporate life today. Following a strong innovation process, and especially this Reflect and Review step, mitigates this risk.

- Unless this step is done well, rumours often emerge which become part of a project's mythology, leading to inaccurate learnings being shared as hard truths within the organization. This most often happens when projects fail, and people try to influence the narrative of what went wrong to deflect blame from themselves or their team. This happens most frequently in more siloed organizations. This is clearly human nature, as no individual or team wants to be perceived as the one who screwed up. However, this is very dangerous as future projects will be influenced by these inaccurate learnings, potentially sending them off-course.

Steps to success

So you've developed and launched your innovative offer, you've understood its performance, and you've got a plan to optimize it. Contrary to thinking that your project is already finished, make sure that you execute this very important final Reflect and Review step to the very best of your ability. Our primary focus here is on lessons learned. The power question for this step:

> **What did we learn and what would we do differently next time?**

As always, there are three sub-steps to help you with this and these should all be done in the context of the frame that you fixed at the very beginning of the project, back in Step 1:

  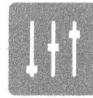

CELEBRATE · CRITIQUE · CALIBRATE

CELEBRATE

However the project has gone, whether well or badly, it is important to take a moment to CELEBRATE. To discuss and formally capture positive achievements.

There will always be some elements of the project, or indeed efforts and contributions of some members of the taskforce team, that can and should be celebrated.

You can use some or all of the following power questions:

> **What went well on this project?**
>
> **What did we do well on this project?**
>
> **What can we be most proud of on this project?**
>
> **What was our most significant breakthrough?**
>
> **What should we keep for our next project?**
>
> **What worked well for us as a team?**

In the case of a project that has gone less well, it is still important to celebrate the fact that you tried. Trying to innovate is a prerequisite for succeeding to innovate. It is also important to recognize that, at the very least, you learned something about your core customers, which means that you are more likely to succeed with a future innovation project. As Nelson Mandela famously said 'I never lose. I either win or learn.'

CRITIQUE

With your taskforce team, discuss and empathize with one another over the difficulties experienced as part of this project. You can use some or all of the following power questions:

What went less well on this project?

What did we do less well on this project?

What can we be most critical of on this project?

What significant roadblocks did we encounter?

What should we stop for our next project?

What worked less well for us as a team?

The objective here is absolutely not to create a finger-pointing blame game – as a mature group of adults, try to have a helicopter view of the project, and review the project objectively.

Be explicit at the start of this discussion that the purpose of this Reflect and Review step is learning, not blaming. If something went wrong, examine the process, not just the people. Reframe difficulties as systemic challenges, rather than personal ones. This will be more or less easy depending on the company culture of your organization, and more difficult in those companies with a very traditional or hierarchical culture.

Even if you feel that the project went really well, don't be tempted to skip over this sub-step, because there will always be useful learnings which can help you with future projects.

Doing this exercise as a project team, rather than individually, brings the significant benefit of allowing all team members to express themselves about what they found tricky, which can be highly therapeutic. Just make sure that the context of these discussions allows each team member to talk safely, with no fear of judgement or retribution for what they may say.

CALIBRATE

Here, your job is to identify those things that need to be changed – either dialled up or dialled down – to maximize the probability of success in future innovative projects. You can use some or all of the following power questions:

> **What should we do differently on our next project?**
>
> **What should we reduce or remove for our next project?**
>
> **What should we improve or increase for our next project?**
>
> **What should we change from a team perspective?**

Try to make each point as specific and actionable as possible, not broad themes. What would you actually *do* differently.

—

As part of the above sub-steps, you will create a lot of very detailed and rich material, all of which should be kept. However, I recommend that you also produce a one-page executive summary. Ideally you will review this with key stakeholders first to ensure that they are aligned, and that all points of view have been covered, before sharing more widely – whether in a formal project review meeting or electronically. This is a very powerful way to close the project and demonstrate your strong leadership until the very end.

Make sure to share these learnings as widely as possible across your organization, focusing on those people who lead similar innovative projects. This will allow them to benefit from your learnings, and therefore for the performance of their projects to increase. Behaviour breeds behaviour, and so this will also help to create a culture where other project leaders share their learnings, thus elevating the innovation performance of the whole organization.

—

Top tips

✓ Animate this step as a plenary discussion with your cross-functional project team, to ensure that you cover all the different angles of the project.

✓ Try to do this session in person rather than online, if possible, as this will encourage people to express themselves more fully and freely.

✓ Ideally, don't have this discussion in your normal office or meeting room as this may make it more difficult for you to take a step back.

- Facilitate this session in an engaging way, for example by using sticky notes, rather than seeing this project review step as just a 'tick the box' or a 'fill the template' exercise.
- Base as much of your discussions as possible on facts, data, metrics and evidence, rather than subjective anecdotes or personal opinion.
- Make sure to capture learnings from the whole project, not just the latter stages. Use the INNOVATOR Way® as a means of reminding you of each step of the project.

Learnings from leaders

Amazon stands out in its rigorous approach to a Reflect and Review mindset. This is embodied in its Correction of Error (COE) process, which is systematically used to manage incidents and failures, whether related to new offers or not.

Some of the elements that I particularly appreciate about Amazon's approach:

- Whilst post-event analysis is part of the COE process, it is different from a post-mortem, because the focus is on corrective actions, not just documenting failures.
- Their focus is not on finding who's to blame for the problem, or to punish them, but rather to enable maximum visibility of those areas that are most in need of improvement.
- Rather than staying at a superficial level of analysis, they use the Five Whys technique (similar to

that which we saw in Step 2, Immerse and Inquire) to drill down to the root causes.

- The core outcome of the COE process is the identification of actionable activities that improve either the prevention, diagnosis or resolution of the root cause of the same problem in the future. Each action item must state its priority, who is the person responsible, and a due date for when it will be finished.

- They proactively transform the learnings from incidents into the Operational Readiness Review (ORR). This consists of checklists for risk assessment which prevent the recurrence of incidents by removing the common causes of issues, thereby helping to achieve operational excellence.

Actions to accelerate

Here are the top three actions to help you move forward:

1. schedule and lead a Reflect and Review session with your taskforce team
2. after the session, consolidate project learnings into an executive summary one-pager, making sure that all taskforce team members agree with this summary and that it is fully representative
3. schedule a session with key project stakeholders to share learnings, before going on to share with other relevant people within your organization who can benefit from your learnings.

PART 3:

INNOVATOR IMPACT

So far in this book, we've covered the foundations of innovation and walked through each step of the INNOVATOR Way®. You are now well equipped to lead and actively contribute to innovation projects – congratulations!

In this final part of the book, we are going to focus on how to maximize your real-world impact when innovating, by looking through four different lenses.

In Chapter 14, 'Situations and solutions', we will cover 10 tricky situations that frequently arise for innovators in companies, and I will propose some topline suggestions on how to best manage these.

In Chapter 15, 'Harness your habits', we will explore how you can maximize your innovation performance as an individual over time, by embracing the power of mini-missions.

In Chapter 16, 'Culture vs. chaos', we will unpack how to boost the innovation culture within your organization.

And finally in Chapter 17, 'Arise and act!', I will summarize and recap the key themes that we have explored throughout this book.

Let's go!

14

Situations and solutions

So far in this book, I have tried to make innovating as simple and straightforward as possible, to help you to make maximum progress. However, unfortunately, innovating is not always plain sailing, and there can be some hurdles and roadblocks along the way.

In this chapter, I will cover 10 of the most common situations that I have encountered in companies and propose some initial solution ideas. Given that each organization is unique, these inputs should not be seen as a magic wand, but rather as helpful pointers and guidance.

'You need to innovate!'

Situation: leaders in your organization say that they want you to innovate, but don't clearly define what that means or what they really want you to do.

Solutions:

✓ Use the power questions from Chapters 1 and 2 to clarify what they mean by innovation, and why it is so important for your organization.

✓ Work through the six sub-steps in Step 1, Fix the Frame, to help specify their expectations and articulate what success looks like for them. You can either draft this yourself, providing them with something tangible to react to, or discuss it together.

✓ Continue to check in with these leaders regularly as you take action, to ensure that your frame remains 100% aligned with the strategy – especially if the leadership team changes.

'Can you manage innovation as well?'

Situation: you are asked to manage innovation on top of your day job, as an additional responsibility to your core role.

Solutions:

✓ First, smile! This situation often happens because leaders think you're capable of taking on more, and it's great that they're trusting you to work on a subject as important as innovation.

✓ Ideally reach a formal agreement on what proportion of your time you will dedicate to innovating, for example one day per week, as well as clarifying which elements of your current work can be deprioritized.

✓ To ensure that this time is protected, it can be helpful to stick to the same day/time every week, potentially working in a different place to separate you from your day job.

'Not our priority right now'

Situation: you need support from people in other teams or functions to move your innovation project forward, but they say it is not high enough priority for them to actively support or resource it.

There can be two underlying reasons for this. First, they may genuinely not perceive it as high enough priority for them, in the context of their other priorities. Or, second, they may not want to support you, due to a sense of rivalry or competition which happens frequently in siloed organizations.

Solutions:

✓ Reinforce how closely linked your innovation project is to overall company strategy, as the stronger the link, the harder it is to challenge strategic importance.

✓ Emphasize what's in it for them, i.e. the opportunity to actively contribute to an exciting and innovative project, which may become high profile within your organization. Ideally you can also link the project to the specific goals and objectives of that team.

✓ Engage and communicate with them right from the beginning of the innovation project, being clear on what specific support you are looking for, rather than waiting until the project is more advanced and you need urgent support.

✓ If they ultimately help you, make sure to visibly acknowledge and celebrate their participation as the project progresses, to boost their enthusiasm to further support you now and in the future.

'You need to follow standard process'

Situation: before an innovative initiative can ever see the light of day, it needs the formal go-ahead from certain functions and teams whose specific role it is to minimize risk for your company. As your innovative project necessarily carries some level of risk, it is normal that they may try to block it or slow it down.

Solutions:

✓ It's all about relationships. Building them, nurturing them, and ensuring that they're mutually beneficial. Make the time and effort to get to know the humans behind the process, and understand what *their* objectives are, what *they* are trying to achieve and why. Do this as early as possible and throughout the life of your project.

✓ Share the frame of your innovation project with them. Unless they understand the 'why', they are unlikely to support you with the 'how'.

✓ If you hit a roadblock regarding validation, use fewer closed questions such as 'Can you...?', and prioritize more open and inclusive questions such as 'How can we...?' as a way of identifying solutions which are feasible and acceptable.

✓ Always anticipate deadlines for which you need their support. Make sure not to spring surprises on them at the last minute, as this not only jeopardizes your project, but will probably also kill a lot of the positive goodwill you have built up.

'No budget to innovate'

Situation: you want to progress an innovative project, but it is difficult to secure budget to move it forward.

Solutions:

✓ Start by working through Steps 1 to 6 of the INNOVATOR Way® (until the point that you may need to do formal customer research), as these don't require any significant budget.

✓ Share your offer idea, and results from your customer tests, in a one-to-one setting with key stakeholders initially to get their feedback. This one-on-one approach can be safer than unveiling it within a group setting where one person's opinion can quickly and negatively influence the whole group.

✓ Remember to bring your offer idea to life for them visually, to help them understand it and get excited. It is typically much easier to unlock budget when stakeholders can see and experience an idea in a tangible way, as they can more easily see how it can create value for customers and the company.

✓ Use their feedback to further refine your proposal, before then presenting it to whoever has the ability to fund your project for the next steps and launch.

'Your budget's been cut'

Situation: the funding for your innovation project gets removed, reduced or reallocated during the project due to financial pressures in the organization or wider economy.

Solutions:

✓ First, show pragmatism and a willingness to make some compromises regarding budget, otherwise it may appear that you have simply not understood that the context has changed.

✓ Show as clearly as possible how your innovation project is going to actively move company strategy and performance forward; i.e. your project is not an optional nice-to-have, but rather a key pillar of future company success.

✓ Break down funding requirements into smaller discrete phases, so that the project can still be approved to move forward to the next stage without stopping completely. This might give you an edge in securing some budget over competing projects.

✓ If there genuinely isn't enough budget available to develop and deliver the project successfully, accept that it might be necessary to stop or postpone it – making sure that you inform key stakeholders that this is happening due to business context.

'I'm not going to risk my bonus...'

Situation: your innovation project is not supported by certain stakeholders or teams in the organization as it might jeopardize their performance targets, bonuses or incentives. This can often arise with more operationally oriented teams such as manufacturing or logistics.

Solutions:

✓ It's important to openly acknowledge that there is a tension between what your innovation project requires for successful implementation, and the targets, bonuses or incentives that are already in place for that team. Don't simply pretend they're not there.

✓ One solution to address this is to try to limit the existing performance targets, bonuses or incentives to the existing business; i.e. the part of the business which is well-established, predictable and optimized – and to exclude more innovative initiatives, which will necessarily be less predictable and less optimized.

✓ Ideally, you will ultimately be able to agree on joint objectives or **key performance indicators** regarding innovation across all of the functional teams that are required to make it happen – as this is the only sustainable way to ensure that everyone is trying to achieve the same innovation goals, with minimal friction.

'Not invented here!'

Situation: your innovation idea is spontaneously rejected by stakeholders or teams, simply because they did not personally create the idea.

Solutions:

- ✓ First, don't take it personally. Whilst not very open-minded, this kind of behaviour is very common and driven by human nature.
- ✓ As suggested above, reinforce how closely linked your innovative initiative is to company strategy, and how well you think it connects to their part of the business and their objectives. In short, highlight what's in it for them.
- ✓ By elevating the discussion to this level, it can render their initial negative feedback irrelevant and unprofessional.

'But we're already successful, why bother?'

Situation: you hear this phrase, which is the equivalent of 'let's change nothing'. This is frequently heard in companies with more of a manufacturing or industrial heritage. Success can breed complacency and a feeling that there is no need or urgency to adapt for the future.

Your company may indeed already be successful; however, this does not remove the need for you to innovate to continue to be successful going forward. Paraphrasing the words of world-renowned leadership thinker Marshall Goldsmith, what got you here won't necessarily get you there.

Just to be clear, I fully understand why this is the case. Especially within large organizations, people are accustomed to the status quo. And to be honest, they often feel very comfortable, which is why they resist new approaches. I call this **innovation inertia**. The risk that innovation inertia can bring to a business, even a long-established successful one, is very real.

Given that the world is constantly moving forward, I often think of businesses as being on a treadmill: you've got to proactively move forward, otherwise you can quickly get thrown off.

Solutions:

✓ Ask the stakeholder(s) who said this to read Chapter 2 of this book.

✓ Gather real-world examples of how your industry is evolving right now. Who are the new and agile players who are offering fresh solutions to your customers' needs? What are startups doing in your industry (however small their business may be today)? What are the new emerging technologies and business models? Make it your responsibility to share these elements to create discussion.

✓ People in large organizations often tend to listen more actively to people who are outside of the organization. So, invite a credible external expert to come and share their views on the future of the industry and what companies should do to anticipate this.

✓ If their resistance is a symptom of not wanting to take risk, you can frame innovation as a means of proactively managing risk instead. Through innovating you are reducing the risk of becoming irrelevant or obsolete. After all, your customers' needs and expectations are evolving – driven by new technology, competitor activity, and their experiences in other industries. Failing to evolve is probably more dangerous than trying something new.

'I just don't like it'

Situation: last but not least, one of the most common innovation killers – the personal opinion!

Often when asked about an innovative idea, the spontaneous response is a personal opinion. In today's world dominated by social media, we've got very used to 'liking' things without a significant amount of thought.

Hopefully the danger from an innovation perspective is obvious. Personal opinions of people inside your company shouldn't matter – what matters is the opinions of your core customers, whether your offer brings them value, and whether they would buy, use or consume it.

Solutions:

✓ Give some context before sharing any innovation ideas with stakeholders. Even if stakeholders know the initiative well, remind them who your core customer is and the innovation insight that you're responding to. If stakeholders don't know the project well, you can also share your frame to give them helpful context about your project from a business perspective.

✓ Especially if you think that your stakeholder may react negatively to your idea, be ready to share real-world evidence from your core customers about what *they* think about your idea, from your Verify the Value step. This could be in the form of research reports, test data, verbatims or video testimonials.

✓ Sometimes stakeholders react negatively not because of the idea per se, but because they simply don't believe that the customer need exists or is significant enough to drive business growth. In which case, make sure to have some real-world evidence and data about the customer need; i.e. just how strongly your core customers want the outcome and just how much they struggle with the obstacles.

✓ Probe the 'no'; i.e. try to identify the specifics of why your stakeholder doesn't like your idea. There could be many potential reasons behind their objections: too risky? Too expensive? Unrealistic growth targets? Not aligned with company strategy? And so on. This clarity allows you to either counter their challenges on the spot or come back to them later once you have refined your idea or your way of explaining it.

—

Whatever situation you encounter, remember that it is never the first time that an innovator has encountered it, and that there is *always* a solution, however desperate it may feel at the time! Try not to see these situations as difficulties or failures, but rather as learning opportunities which will help you become a better and more confident innovator. Just like someone who practises martial arts like judo or karate, you grow through adversity, and become stronger thanks to the struggle, not in spite of it.

15

Harness your habits

Much excellent work has recently been written about the power of habits, i.e. the huge benefits which can be gained from compounding small, consistent and incremental improvements over time. For me, the eureka moment from this work was from James Clear, the author of *Atomic Habits*: 'if you can get just 1 percent better each day, you'll end up with results that are nearly 37 times better after one year.'[1]

This principle applies brilliantly to becoming a better innovator. Yes, you will become a better innovator if you lead and participate in innovation projects. However, you will become an even greater innovator if you integrate innovator mini-missions as a daily habit.

Innovator mini-missions are a really quick and easy way of becoming a 1% better innovator every day. Just to be clear, I'm absolutely not suggesting adding big tasks on top of your already heavy workload, but rather tiny micro-actions which can easily be integrated into the busiest of schedules.

---

[1] 1% better every day for one year: $1.01^{365} = 37.78$

Here is an initial list of 30 suggestions to help you get started. This list is not designed to be exhaustive nor prescriptive. These suggestions are organized by step of the INNOVATOR Way®, to enable you to boost your innovator performance throughout the full innovation process. However, it is fully up to you to decide where you would like to start, and in which order to do them:

Fix the Frame:

⇒ try to figure out the growth goal behind a new offer you saw that just launched
⇒ during a project meeting, ask the team to recap exactly why you are doing this project
⇒ stick a one-page summary of your core customer profile next to your desk.

Immerse and Inquire:

⇒ buy and use your company's offer, capturing and sharing your experience
⇒ ask your customer careline team for the top query or complaint from last week
⇒ go shopping in the favourite retail or online stores of your core customer.

Narrow the Need:

⇒ craft an innovation insight from a moment when you were recently really frustrated
⇒ try to figure out the innovation insight for a recent launch in another industry

⇒ share an innovation insight with a core customer in your network to see if it resonates.

Nail a Northstar:

⇒ think of a competitor launch, and guess what their 'How Might We...?' might have been
⇒ write a 'How Might We...?' question using a benchmark brand from another industry
⇒ find a 'How Might We...?' example online and rewrite it to make it more ambitious.

Open up Options:

⇒ quickly create 10 new offer ideas for your company, no matter how small or crazy
⇒ think of an offer your company launched, and generate three alternative offer ideas
⇒ take an innovation success from another industry and ask how you can capitalize on it.

Verify the Value:

⇒ think of an offer from your company and identify how you would have prototyped it
⇒ devise a fast, cheap experiment you could have done when developing your last offer
⇒ ask a core customer to rate the degree to which your offer brings them value [0–10].

Achieve the Ambition:

⇒ based on your core customer, identify one additional place you could sell your offer

⇒ follow the most popular social media accounts for your core customers
⇒ look at some outdoor advertising in the street and evaluate what it does well or badly.

Track the Traction:

⇒ call a member of the sales team to ask them how your product or service is performing
⇒ go online and find three recent customer reviews of one of your products or services
⇒ pop into a retail store where your products are sold and observe customers' behaviour.

Optimize the Offer:

⇒ ask a core customer in your network how they would improve your product or service
⇒ identify three ways you could potentially improve your worst-selling product or service
⇒ ask yourself how you would improve your offer if it were your own business.

Reflect and Review:

⇒ identify a recent success in your current project and share it with the team
⇒ at the end of today, ask yourself what you did well, less well and what to change
⇒ ask a project stakeholder for one suggestion on how you can improve future projects.

If you would like some support to get started with mini-missions, why not join my 30 day INNOVATOR Challenge? You will receive a short video in your inbox every day for a month, giving you a fun innovator mini-mission to complete. You can start the challenge at any time, and it is completely free of charge. Consider it my way of helping you take action after reading this book.

Sign up takes less than 30 seconds, by either flashing the QR code below, or by going to **InnovatorChallenge.com**

I hope to see you there!

16

Culture vs. chaos

In this chapter, we're going to explore innovation culture. If you are in an executive, senior or leadership role, with the ability to impact company or team culture, please read on: I wrote this chapter with you in mind. If not, this chapter should still be interesting for you, but maybe less actionable right now – in which case, please feel free to skip directly to the final chapter.

To truly maximize the innovation impact of an organization requires a high-performing innovation culture, as opposed to innovation chaos. Clearly the culture of any organization is bigger than any one individual, and you will certainly not be able to change the culture of your organization on your own.

My objective of exploring this topic here is twofold. First, to help you identify how strong or weak the innovation culture of your organization currently is. This will help you better understand why innovative projects proceed smoothly, or indeed why they sometimes feel like pushing water up a hill. Second, I want to share some helpful pointers regarding what can be done to boost your company's innovation culture, based on my real-life experiences.

Whilst many organizations put a significant focus and energy on creating individual innovation projects, those innovation projects are significantly less likely to succeed if they are not managed in a culture and environment which actively nurtures innovation. It's like gardening: you can try to grow tomatoes, for example, but without a supportive environment with the heat, the light and the water they need, they are certainly not going to grow very large, and most likely will simply shrivel and die.

When many people think about innovation culture, they think of it as being something that's quite vague and intangible, something that is almost too big to get your arms around. However, I see it much more simply than that. For me, an innovation culture is a culture which motivates people to innovate, by providing them with what they *need* to innovate. And, for me, the best tool to help identify people's needs is still Maslow's hierarchy of needs, which is often depicted in the form of a pyramid.

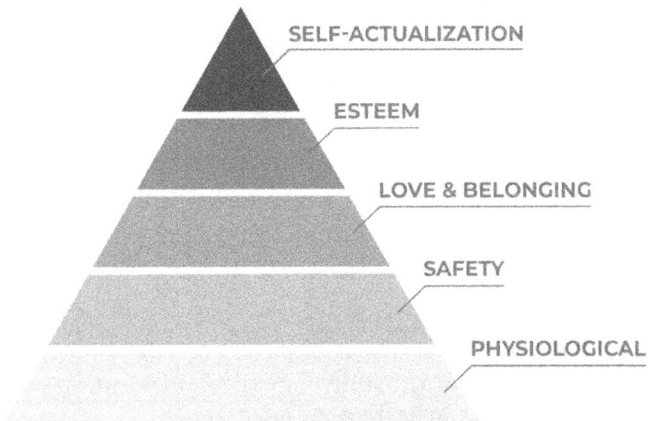

Whilst this framework may now be over 80 years old, it's as relevant today as it was back then. I'm sure that you're already familiar with it, but here's a quick recap just in case. Maslow was an American psychologist who stated that humans are motivated by a hierarchy of needs. In this hierarchy, human needs are organized such that the largest, most basic needs are at the bottom of the pyramid and must be satisfied before people start to fulfil the needs on the next level up.

As we're trying to identify what people *need* to innovate, this framework can be relevantly and successfully applied to innovation culture. Let's work through it level by level.

Physiological needs

At the very bottom of the pyramid, we have physiological needs. These are the absolute basics that someone who is innovating in an organization needs. They need some knowledge and skills on how to innovate (reading this book is definitely a strong start!), and ideally also some training to help put this knowledge and these skills into practice.

Innovators need to be empowered to move innovative projects forward, so that their efforts are not challenged or blocked at every turn. In practice, this means that there must be active and explicit senior leadership support for innovation, beyond a tacit acceptance that innovation is necessary.

Innovation must also be formalized in relevant roles and reward structures in the organization, otherwise this sends a clear message that it is not a strategic priority.

The resources required to innovate should be easily accessible. For example, ideally, taskforce teams will have a dedicated space to easily collaborate, leaving project materials stuck on the wall, rather than wasting time and energy booking meeting rooms for one-hour slots, and needing to tidy up project materials every time.

Ideally, each innovation project would be allocated a meeting room for its own private use from day 1 of the project, right until project closure; this was a tip that I gained from visiting iconic innovation consultancy IDEO in their San Francisco office.

Also at this level, innovators need to have a deep and direct understanding of their customers and get regular inspiration and stimulation from outside the company, for example on trends and competitors.

So those are some of the most basic and fundamental innovator needs. It is possible that these needs may not yet be fully satisfied in your organization. Addressing these is the very first place to start when building an innovation culture. Once these needs have been addressed, then we can move up to the safety needs.

Safety needs

This level is critical if we want people to dare to innovate within an organization. We need to ensure that our team members feel like they are in a safe space: that they feel safe to ask questions, feel safe to try new things, feel safe to take some risks, and feel safe if their innovation project doesn't work out.

Without this feeling of safety, unsurprisingly, people are very reluctant to innovate because of the risk that it could damage their reputation, their career prospects, or even their job security. Simply put, it must be safe to fail.

In many organizations, unfortunately, there is still a systemic negative judgement of the project leader or project team if an innovative project fails. If they have done a poor job on the project and have not rigorously followed a robust innovation method, then fair enough. However, if they have rigorously followed an innovation process, and they have simply not found a way to get the project to work, then they should be celebrated for being brave enough to stand up and say so prior to launch, thus saving the company a lot of time, energy and money.

Remember that an innovation funnel (sometimes known as an innovation pipeline) is so-called because there should be many more ideas explored than the company will ultimately launch, so it is completely normal that some projects are killed along the way. Only the strongest projects should survive, meaning that your company should only end up launching those with the highest probability of moving the company towards its strategic goals.

Beware if your innovation funnel effectively becomes an innovation tunnel, where there is an expectation that every project will proceed to launch with success, as this is often a sign that either not enough ideas are being explored, or that project prioritization is not strong enough.

One powerful and practical tip which I have seen work really well in building safety in an organization:

encourage senior stakeholders to share stories about innovative projects they have led which did not work. This reinforces that they have still become successful despite those project failures.

Love and belonging needs

Once we have addressed safety needs, we can move up to the love and belonging needs. Within the context of corporate innovation, this is all about the need to feel like you belong, that you're part of a group. It's the need for interpersonal relationships, the need for connection.

Too often I observe that people who innovate in large organizations feel quite isolated, feel alone, feel like a misfit or an outsider, or feel like they're on a mission without necessarily the full support of the organization or their peers. This is clearly pretty sad and must absolutely be fixed if we want to build a strong innovation culture.

In my experience, there are two powerful things you can do here to help deliver against the needs at this level. First, ensure that innovators have support such as a senior sponsor, mentor or coach within the organization, but outside their direct hierarchy. Someone they can turn to for advice or support when things get tough.

Second, it can also be hugely beneficial to be part of an external community of innovator peers. Every time I gather a group of innovators together, whether in person or online, there is always an immediate spark and connection between them. There is a huge sense of belonging and solidarity, given that people quickly discover that they are all facing almost identi-cal innovation challenges, despite being in different companies and different industries.

Esteem needs

Once these love and belonging needs are satisfied, we move up to the esteem level. This level is all about getting respect and recognition from others for what you do. It's about gaining self-esteem and confidence.

For people innovating in large organizations, this means acknowledging, rewarding and celebrat-ing success – and not just at the end of an innovation project, as this doesn't happen very frequently, but rather every time you see someone is doing some-thing positive in line with the innovation culture that you want to build. This not only motivates the specific individual but also creates a halo effect which posi-tively influences other team members.

The executive or leadership team has a critical role to play here to ensure that they are not just say-ing that they value innovation but actually demon-strating this through actions. Creating high-visibility innovation awards in the company can be a relatively simple, yet effective solution here.

Self-actualization needs

Once the esteem needs have been addressed, we move up to the final level, self-actualization. Self-actu-alization is the desire to accomplish everything you can and become the best that you can be. This level is all about the realization of someone's potential as an innovator, about them maximizing personal growth, and achieving peak innovation performance.

In my experience, at this level, innovators need specific support which can rarely be found within their organization. They are a bit like high-level athletes: they need tailored support to help them reach peak performance. A more generic, generalist or basic approach will not be good enough to help achieve their full potential.

This is where tailored innovation coaching with a senior experienced corporate innovator outside the organization can be really helpful, as they can bring both the innovation expertise and an objective external perspective.

At this level, innovators also have another important role to play: to actively support others within their organization who are less far along their innovation journey, by acting as a mentor. This is their moment to give back and contribute to building a bigger innovator movement and legacy.

—

So hopefully you now see how Maslow's hierarchy of needs can help us to identify not only the actions to build innovation culture, but also the order in which to do them. One important point: the actions that you put in place should be part of an ongoing action plan to build innovation culture. It is always much more effective to do several smaller actions consistently over time, than a smaller number of ad hoc big bang actions, the effect of which often doesn't last very long.

As innovation culture grows, even if slowly, it sweeps like a wave through the organization, resulting in a much wider population adopting more innovative approaches: asking better questions, exploring new possibilities, trying and testing new things. The company culture starts to foster innovation, rather than rely on just a few individuals, and the innovation wave grows in size and intensity, leading to better business performance.

If all of these innovation culture elements are not yet in place in your organization, even those addressing more basic physiological needs, please don't despair. There are not so many companies where they *are* all in place! Certainly don't be discouraged from proceeding with your innovation projects. Action brings progress, progress brings results, and results help to boost your innovator confidence, and the innovation culture of the whole organization.

17

Arise and act!

So that's it! I hope this book has delivered on my promise to give you a step-by-step guide to becoming a successful innovator. The 10 simple steps of the INNOVATOR Way® will help and guide you to create and launch innovative offers with success.

Beyond that, I hope that it will help you to actively boost the five INNOVATOR 'SCORE' behaviours that you encountered when you completed the INNOVATOR Scorecard in Chapter 3. These five behaviours underpin the 10 steps of the INNOVATOR Way®, and enable me to neatly summarize the five key themes we've explored in this book:

S = Strategy-sharp:

[These behaviours underpin the Fix the Frame step]

✓ being clear on a strong company strategy – whether you are responsible for writing it or executing it
✓ being able to clearly articulate how projects and decisions contribute towards achieving company strategy
✓ helping your team and colleagues to see how their work actively helps to achieve company strategy.

C = Customer-curious:

[These behaviours underpin the Immerse and Inquire and Narrow the Need steps]

✓ being able to clearly describe who your core customers are, what they want and need, and what they struggle with
✓ getting out of the office to meet directly with customers in their real environment, rather than relying only on reports or assumptions
✓ committing to take action on customer learnings to improve your work, products, services and solutions.

O = Opportunity-oriented:

[These behaviours underpin the Nail a Northstar and Open up Options steps]

✓ systematically exploring multiple possible solutions, rather than jumping on the first or most obvious idea
✓ proactively bringing fresh ideas to your team or business, even if they challenge the status quo
✓ actively listening and considering new ideas from others, rather than dismissing them too quickly.

R = Reality-rooted:

[These behaviours underpin the Verify the Value and Achieve the Ambition steps]

✓ going beyond desk research, and testing new ideas with real customers as early as possible, rather than waiting to have the perfect solution

✓ deeply understanding where your core customers shop, and which media they love to consume

✓ committing to move projects from business idea to real-life execution, to unlock the value for customers and the company.

E = Execution-elevating:

[These behaviours underpin the Track the Traction, Optimize the Offer and Reflect and Review steps]

✓ regularly tracking real-world results of projects to determine if they are achieving the objectives and intended impact

✓ proactively looking for ways to improve what your company offers, whether products, services, solutions or customer experience

✓ dedicating sufficient time and energy to conduct project reviews, sharing learnings widely to maximize business benefits in the future.

Even if you don't currently lead innovation projects as a core part of your job, make sure to continue to demonstrate and nurture these five INNOVATOR 'SCORE' behaviours. Not only will they help you to become a better innovator, but they will also make you a better business leader. Research clearly demonstrates that it is exactly these types of behaviours which are most required in the workplace of today and tomorrow.

Before we close

In my view, there has never been a more exciting time to be an innovator, and I hope that reading this book has inspired you to take action. As I wrote in the Introduction, don't try to do everything at once. Start with one step. Test out a few of the tools and techniques. As the quote commonly attributed to former US President Harry S. Truman neatly summarizes: 'Imperfect action is better than perfect inaction'.

Please stay in touch and let me know how you get on. Yes, really! You can reach me via email at **tom@innovatorbook.com**

Nothing gives me greater pleasure than hearing about concrete actions and business results that have stemmed from the INNOVATOR Way®. And I'll happily include your success stories in the second edition of this book.

If you would like support putting the INNOVATOR Way® into action, either as an individual or more widely in your organization, please go to **innovinco.com** for details of our products and services.

In short, arise and act, and let's make the world a better place through innovation.

Tom Pullen
July 2025

P.S. Please can I ask a favour?

If you have found this book helpful, please help me by taking just one minute right now to leave a quick review. A rating, or even just a few words, would mean the world to me, and will enable this book to reach and help more people.

Regardless of where you bought it (and even if it was gifted to you), please flash the QR code below, or go to **InnovatorBookReview.com**

Thanks in advance for your support!

Acknowledgements

This book would not have happened without the help and contributions of many people, over many years, for which I am truly grateful.

First, thanks to all those colleagues and collaborators who inspired and coached me in innovation, marketing and customer-centric growth during my 18 years on the corporate side, working at Boots, Mars and Danone. The amount I learned from you is immeasurable.

Thanks to the trustees of the Nottingham Roosevelt Memorial Travelling Scholarship which I was privileged to win in 2001. This US-based programme gave me the unique opportunity to exchange with iconic companies such as Nike, P&G and Kodak, and made me understand the value of hands-on company research, which has been the approach for this book.

Thanks to the d.school team at Stanford University for opening my eyes to the power of Design Thinking in Hong Kong back in 2016. That programme fundamentally changed my perspective on innovation and remains one of the highlights of my career.

Thanks to the teams at HEC Paris for their incredible support – not only helping me succeed with my Executive MBA but also selecting Innovinco® for their very first Incubator cohort at Station F, the world's largest startup campus. This offered invaluable learning about startup innovation techniques. I'm also grateful to the Executive Education team for frequently inviting me to teach innovation to company executives, which is always engaging and enjoyable.

Thanks to all the great companies I've had the privilege of working with over the past eight years. Each of them has taught me something valuable about how to innovate successfully and has allowed me to exchange with some brilliant people.

Thanks to my business coaching group led by Chris Ducker, with fellow authors including Advita Patel, Becca Pountney, Jenni Field and Rich Birch. Thanks for being at the genesis of this book. Thanks also to Christian Baker for encouraging me to just get on with it.

Thank you to the beta readers who selflessly gave so much time and expertise to review the initial manuscript, and whose contributions have made it much better than it would otherwise have been: Arnaud Lecharny, Aurélie Roche, Dominica Parry, Frédéric Jouin, Londa Rebetzke, Marc Gillmann, Maxime Maignan, Melina Galeadi, Olga Guerous, Ollie Banks, Paul Tisdale, Rémy Peugniez, Roisin Kirby and Stéphane Renard. Thanks also to Ginny whose manuscript feedback was invaluable, especially regarding the Introduction.

Thank you to my trusted team at Crea Nostra – Matthieu Vinel, Claire Amilhat and Mafe Ariza – for creating the cover and the many visuals in this book. And to the hugely talented Béatrice Urseau who drew all of the illustrations for Chapter 14. It is always a privilege to collaborate with you.

A massive thank you to the whole team at Practical Inspiration Publishing who have worked tirelessly to get this book out into the world, and across the world. A heartfelt thank you to Alison Jones for awarding me a publishing deal based on my initial book proposal, giving me the confidence I needed to go ahead and write it.

Last but not least, I am hugely grateful to my wonderful wife, Louise, and our fantastic kids Josh, Sam, Sophie and Dan. You have shown immense amounts of patience over the past two years I have been writing this book and provided so much inspiration and support. Thank you.

Glossary

Access: to facilitate customer purchase through convenient points of distribution

Activate: to drive customer excitement and engagement through experiential communication

B2C (Business-to-Consumer): when businesses sell offers directly to individual consumers

B2B (Business-to-Business): when businesses sell offers to other businesses

Beneficiary: the customer who uses and gains the greatest value from an offer

Buyer: the customer who purchases an offer

Core customer: the primary customer profile a business aims to serve with an offer

Customer clues: raw information and observations that help to better understand customers, their desired outcomes and obstacles they face

Frame: the goals and scope that guide where a project will and won't focus, and how it will proceed

Growth goal: the customer behaviour an innovation project aims to change, and the level of change targeted

Innovation inertia: the resistance within an organization, team or individuals that slows or blocks new ideas and change

Innovation insight: the articulation of the gap between what the customer wants or needs (outcome) and the pains they face to achieve it (obstacles), which can be actioned to drive business growth

Innovator energy: the positivity, optimism, dynamism, proactivity and agility needed to innovate successfully

Key performance indicators (KPIs): specific metrics used to track progress towards goals

Message: the primary idea communicated about your offer to inspire customers to buy, use or consume it

Media: the communication channels and touchpoints most likely to reach your core customers and drive behaviour change

Northstar: an ambitious 'How Might We...?' question that inspires the generation of a large number of ambitious ideas

Obstacle: a pain, problem or frustration a customer experiences when trying to achieve an outcome

Offer: a product, service or solution designed to help core customers to achieve an outcome more easily

Outcome: an end result a customer wants or needs to achieve

Power questions: key questions that guide innovation projects towards successful results

Required resources: the budget and materials without which the taskforce team is not confident of project success

Stakeholder strategy: the identification of key project stakeholders and how they will be proactively managed

Strategic scope: a specific area of focus for a project which is driven by company strategy

Taskforce team: a temporary, action-oriented team set up to develop and deploy a specific innovation project

Bibliography

Bland, David J., and Alexander Osterwalder. *Testing Business Ideas.* John Wiley & Sons, Inc, 2020.

Bryar, Colin, and Bill Carr. *Working Backwards: Insights, Stories, and Secrets from inside Amazon.* St. Martin's Press, 2021.

Catmull, Edwin E., and Amy Wallace. *Creativity, Inc: Overcoming the Unseen Forces That Stand in the Way of True Inspiration.* Random House, 2014.

Clear, James. *Atomic Habits: Tiny Changes, Remarkable Results; an Easy & Proven Way to Build Good Habits & Break Bad Ones.* Avery, 2018.

Covey, Stephen R., and James C. Collins. *The 7 Habits of Highly Effective People: Powerful Lessons in Personal Change.* Revised and updated edition. Simon & Schuster, 2020.

Decker, Charles L. *P & G 99: 99 Principles and Practices of Procter and Gamble's Success.* HarperCollins, 1998.

Doorley, Scott, and Scott Witthoft. *Make Space: How to Set the Stage for Creative Collaboration.* John Wiley & Sons, 2012.

Dweck, Carol. *Mindset: The New Psychology of Success: How We Can Learn to Fulfill Our Potential: Parenting, Business, School, Relationships.* Random House Publishing Group, 2016.

Frier, Sarah. *No Filter: The Inside Story of How Instagram Transformed Business, Celebrity and Our Culture.* Random House Business, 2020.

Gallagher, Leigh. *The Airbnb Story: How Three Ordinary Guys Disrupted an Industry, Made Billions… and Created Plenty of Controversy.* First Mariner Books edition, Houghton Mifflin Harcourt, 2018.

Harvard Business Review, Clayton M. Christensen, Theodore Levitt, Philip Kotler and Fred Reichheld. *HBR's 10 Must Reads on Strategic Marketing (with Featured Article Marketing Myopia, by Theodore Levitt).* Harvard Business Review Press, 2013.

Hastings, Reed, and Erin Meyer. *No Rules Rules: Netflix and the Culture of Reinvention.* WH Allen, 2020.

Iger, Robert. *The Ride of a Lifetime: Lessons Learned from 15 Years as CEO of the Walt Disney Company.* Random House, 2019.

Isaacson, Walter. *Elon Musk.* Simon & Schuster, 2023.

Isaacson, Walter. *Steve Jobs.* Simon & Schuster, 2013.

Keeley, Larry, Helen Walters, Ryan Pikkel and Brian Quinn. *Ten Types of Innovation: The Discipline of Building Breakthroughs.* J. Wiley & Sons, 2013.

Kim, W. Chan, and Renée Mauborgne. *Blue Ocean Strategy: How to Create Uncontested Market Space and Make the Competition Irrelevant.* Harvard Business School Press, 2007.

Knapp, Jake, John Zeratsky and Braden Kowitz. *Sprint: How to Solve Big Problems and Test New Ideas in Just Five Days.* Bantam Press, 2016.

Knight, Philip H. *Shoe Dog: A Memoir by the Creator of Nike.* Scribner, 2016.

Kroc, Ray. *Grinding It Out: The Making of McDonald's.* St. Martin's Paperbacks, 1987.

Lafley, A. G., and Roger L. Martin. *Playing to Win: How Strategy Really Works.* Harvard Business Review Press, 2013.

Lehmann-Ortega, Laurence, Hélène Musikas and Jean-Marc Schoettl. *(Re)Invent Your Business Model: With the Odyssey 3.14 Approach.* Dunod, 2022.

Manly, J., Ringel, M., MacDougall, A., Harnoss, J., Wolke-Perten, J., Backler, W., Gjerstad, K., Kimura, R. and Viner, B. *Innovation Systems Need a Reboot.* Boston Consulting Group, 2024.

Maslow, A. H. 'A Theory of Human Motivation'. *Psychological Review*, vol. 50, no. 4, July 1943.

Nadella, Satya, Greg Shaw, Jill Tracie Nichols and Bill Gates. Foreword. In *Hit Refresh: The Quest to Rediscover Microsoft's Soul and Imagine a Better Future for Everyone.* Harper Business, 2017.

Nooyi, Indra. *My Life in Full: Work, Family, and Our Future.* Portfolio, 2021.

Osterwalder, Alexander and Yves Pigneur. *Business Model Generation: A Handbook for Visionaries, Game Changers, and Challengers.* Wiley, 2010.

Osterwalder, Alexander. *Value Proposition Design: How to Create Products and Services Customers Want.* John Wiley & Sons, 2014.

Randolph, Marc. *That Will Never Work: The Birth of Netflix and the Amazing Life of an Idea.* First edition, Little, Brown and Company, 2019.

Richardson, Tracey M., and Ernie Richardson. *The Toyota Engagement Equation: How to Understand and Implement Continuous Improvement Thinking in Any Organization.* McGraw-Hill Education, 2017.

Ries, Eric. *The Lean Startup: How Constant Innovation Creates Radically Successful Businesses.* Penguin Business, 2019.

Robertson, David, and Bill Breen. *Brick by Brick: How LEGO Rewrote the Rules of Innovation and Conquered the Global Toy Industry.* Crown Business, 2013.

Schmidt, Eric and Jonathan Rosenberg. *How Google Works.* Murray, 2015.

Schultz, Howard, and Dori Jones Yang. *Pour Your Heart into It: How Starbucks Built a Company One Cup at a Time.* Hyperion, 1997.

Schultz, Howard, and Joanne L. Gordon. *Onward: How Starbucks Fought for Its Life without Losing Its Soul.* Wiley, 2011.

Sinek, Simon. *Start with Why: How Great Leaders Inspire Everyone to Take Action.* Portfolio, 2009.

Stone, Brad. *The Everything Store: Jeff Bezos and the Age of Amazon.* Back Bay Books/Little, Brown and Company, 2018.

Syed, Matthew. *Rebel Ideas: The Power of Diverse Thinking.* John Murray, 2019.

Ulwick, Anthony W. *Jobs to Be Done: Theory to Practice.* Idea Bite Press, 2016.

Utley, Jeremy, and Perry Klebahn. *Ideaflow: The Only Business Metric That Matters.* Penguin Publishing Group, 2022.

Vance, Ashlee. *Elon Musk: How the Billionaire CEO of SpaceX and Tesla Is Shaping Our Future.* Virgin Books, 2016.

For more of my innovation book recommendations, head over to **InnovatorReads.com**

Online references

Last accessed and verified in June 2025:
airbnb.com
amazon.com
designsprintkit.withgoogle.com
gv.com/sprint
lego.com
mcdonalds.com
microsoft.com
netflix.com
pg.com
redbull.com
starbucks.com
toyota.com
unilever.com
weforum.org
wikipedia.org
wired.com

About the author

Tom Pullen is CEO of Innovinco®, a company that helps large corporations to maximize business growth by accelerating innovation. Or, as *The Sunday Times* put it, 'helping big companies be more innovative'.

Tom spent the first 18 years of his career driving business growth inside major companies including Boots, Mars and Danone, where he became Global Innovation Director.

Since founding Innovinco® in 2017, he has had the privilege of helping over 30 of the world's leading companies to accelerate innovation performance. These include Danone, Essilor, Estée Lauder, Givaudan, Henkel, L'Oréal, La Poste, LVMH, McCain, Michelin, Pernod Ricard, Quiksilver, Reckitt, Rexel, Schlumberger, The Coca-Cola Company, Toyota, Unilever and Veolia.

Tom trained in Design Thinking at Stanford University, and in Innovative Management at Babson College near Boston. He holds an Executive MBA with Innovation major from HEC Paris, frequently ranked Europe's number one business school, where he now regularly teaches innovation to executives.

He is an award-winning keynote and TEDx speaker who regularly shares practical expertise on innovation via LinkedIn, TV, podcasts, radio and the press.

Tom lives in France, near the Palace of Versailles, with his wife and their four children. He enjoys baguettes, cheese and wine – and does just enough gym and tennis to keep his doctor moderately reassured.

tomjpullen.com

linkedin.com/in/tomjpullen

Index